THE
CHRISTIAN
HOME

By Norman V. Williams

MOODY PRESS
CHICAGO

Printed in the United States of America

CONTENTS

1

THE CHRISTIAN HUSBAND

Ephesians 5:25-33

"Husbands, Love Your Wives"

THE WIFE is subject to the husband, and he is subject to her in love; she to his government and he to her heart; she to his rule and he to her need. In the seventeenth century, Pastor Byfield said of wives, "Nature makes her a woman; election, a wife; but only grace can make her subject." We could say of husbands, "Nature makes him a man; election, a husband; but only grace can fill his heart with the love of Christ."

I. The Pattern—"Even as Christ also loved the church and gave himself for it."

The love of Christ for the Church is to be the pattern of man's love to his wife. No man could ever love his wife to the extent that Christ loves His Church; but all saved husbands can love their wives according to the same pattern. Meyer beautifully says this command "is the sacred refrain of the whole Christian ethics of marriage." Pulsford, that great evangelical scholar of over a half century ago says, "If the love of Christ to the church is the pattern of a husband's love to his wife, his love must rather spring from what he can do for her, rather than from what she is to him." Olshausen in his commentary on Ephesians 5, says, "Christ's love was a self-devoting, self-sacrificing love which had for its object the sanctification of the church. This self-sacrificing, sanctifying love Paul requires of husbands in marriage. True, the wife ought to practice this kind of love to her husband, but the positive influence must always proceed from the man—therefore the commandment."

To possess, manifest, and impart this love is man's special privilege and responsibility in marriage. It is his chief function.

Hodges, that prince of theologians and expositors, brings out four distinguishing characteristics of Christ's love to His Church. It is:

1. Peculiar—Christ has a special, peculiar love for His Bride.

2. Exclusive—Christ has an exclusive possession of His Bride.

3. Intimate—His union with His Bride is more intimate than His relationship with any other portion or part of His creation. We are His Body.

4. Delightful—The Church [author's note: By Church we mean that those who have received Him as their personal Saviour are made members of His Body which is the one, true Church] is the special object of delight to Christ.

These four characteristics should mark and be fully exemplified in the husband's love for his wife.

There are two great Christian streams of thought on the meaning of love. They are not contradictory but supplementary, and both are true to the Word of God. They approach the meaning of Christ—like love from different directions—and they stress different elements in its nature.

Thomas Aquinas emphasizes the element of giving. For him, to love is to give, to will and desire the good of the beloved. A lover's happiness is not found alone in his own satisfaction, but most of all in the happiness of the one he loves. His love takes him out of himself and into the needs, desires, and personality of his beloved. It is a generous and

6

unselfish love. The husband possessing the love of Christ seeks not to take for himself but to give of himself.

We can see in the Word of God how the love of Christ meant giving. All that He became and all that He did and all that He does are for us. He was willing to go all the way to the cross and there to suffer our death that we might live. Such, in pattern, is the giving, self-sacrificing love which the Christian husband bears in his heart toward his beloved.

Augustine emphasizes mainly the desire of the lover to be one with his beloved. Love creates a void in the heart that can be filled only by the beloved. Thus the lover is ever seeking a closer union of heart and life with his beloved. The lover no longer sees his happiness in terms of himself but now only in terms of union with his beloved and both in Christ. There in that union of the two in the Third (Christ) is the meaning and fulfillment of life realized. Thus all the Christian husband does is a seeking for deeper unity with his beloved in thought, word and deed; and with the Lord Jesus Christ through whom the union is made, established, and sustained.

Certainly the love of Christ was a love that longed for union. He died for us not only that we might be pardoned of our sins, but that we might be united with Him forever.

In John 17 our Lord prayed for the unity of believers with each other and with God (John 17:11, 20, 21). And when our Lord ascended into heaven He loved us so much that He gave us the Holy Spirit that we might yet be united with Him!

One has said, "A generous love, a love of giving, that gave to the last drop of the God-Man's blood; a love of unity finding realization in the oneness even of members in a spiritual Body of which He is the Head, His Church! This is what is meant by the love of Christ for His Church."

7

And indeed, this is the love Paul did not hesitate to call the model of the love of husband and wife.

In a study of this kind it is important to notice the word used to denote the love which should exist between husband and wife.

The Greek language had in use three words to denote what we call love.

Storgē is one of these words, and it represents parental and filial affection or what one has called "tender emotion." This word is not used in the New Testament except in derivative forms.

Philia is the second word and it denotes the love of friends, or friendship; this word is occasionally found in the New Testament in its compounds such as *philadelphia* (brotherly love) and *philanthropia* (kindness or love toward man in general); in Titus 2:4 it is used (in compound forms) of love of children and of husband. In Romans 12:10 the word *philostorgoi* (combining *philas* and *storgē*) refers to the warmth of family affection within the Christian brotherhood.

Thirdly there is *eros*. This word refers to love in a physical sense. The word is not found in the New Testament.

Those who translated the Hebrew Scriptures into Greek, about two centuries before Christ, made occasional use of the word *agapē* to denote love in a religious (spiritual) sense—the love of God for man, or of man for God, or of man for man under inspiration of God. Outside the Word of God this word is very rare, but is found often in classical Greek in the form of the verb *agapao*, implying deep, spiritual affection rather than passion, a love which is manifested in practical acts of kindness. The Early Church, under inspiration of the Holy Spirit, fastened upon the word *agapē*. In the New Testament it is used primarily of God's love for man, as shown, taught, and revealed by the Lord Jesus Christ; but it is used likewise of man's love for God and also of his love for his fellow men in and through Christ. For Christians it is the ultimate description of the nature of God. Thus it signified a far deeper and more spiritual love than *storgē*, or tender emotion; than *philia*, human friendship; or *eros*, physical passion. It is always filled with a content and meaning drawn directly from the idea of the love of God which our Lord Jesus Christ has revealed in His life and death. It is significant to note that it is this word which Paul uses when he, under inspiration of the Holy Spirit, commands husbands to love their wives. It means nothing less than that quality of the divine love with which Christ loves the Church. It is upon the enduring and indestructible nature of such love that the husband builds his spiritual ministry to his wife. For her obedience to his rule she is to receive *agapē* love in all the possible ways the Holy Spirit will reveal to the earnest husband.

Agapē love is not an affair of the emotions only, but is an activity of the whole personality, including the will. The world is seeking to build marriage on *eros* love. This is an unstable foundation, as unstable as the passions and attractions upon which it is founded, as is revealed by the present divorce rate.

II. The Aims and Objectives of the Husband's Love

This love of the husband, that which is ever seeking to give itself for the beloved and ever seeking to be identified with the beloved, is to the end of definite spiritual aims and objectives. Christ loved the Church and gave Himself for it that He might:

1. Sanctify and cleanse it
2. Present it to Himself a glorious Church—not having spot or wrinkle

3. That it should be holy and without blemish. The work of Christ is to the end that the Church may be set apart for Him, cleansed, glorified and made holy.

William Kelly in his work on Ephesians says that these blessings are positionally secured to us when we trust Christ as our Saviour, and they are constantly being experimentally appropriated to us by the High Priestly intercessory work of the Lord Jesus Christ on the right hand of the Father's throne. Now the husband is vitally, responsibly and especially related to this High Priestly work of Christ to his wife. The husband's love then becomes a channel of graces and helps to the wife which minister to her growth in grace (sanctification) and anticipates her glorification when she will have consummated her day-by-day growth by the vision of Christ. He is literally to be a fountain of graces and encouragements to his wife. He is to be a vital channel in Christ's High Priestly work to his wife. The husband's joy is to cherish and bless his wife.

The husband is the head of the family. The Church tells him this the day of his wedding, and, if he will only listen, she tells him this all the rest of his life. She tells him with a confidence that stems directly from Christ and from his great apostle Paul. As head of the family, the dignity and authority are his. Much more important, though, is his responsibility to bring the whole family, wife and children, to the feet of Christ.

If a man does this with a full acknowledgment of his own frailty and a childlike reliance on Christ, he will accomplish the two great goals of his life: he will become pleasing to Christ, and pleasing to his wife.

This spiritual ministry of the husband includes the whole of his life. All he does is to be a means of spiritual blessing and growth to his wife. He will not only expound the Word of God to his wife and pray with her, but he will strive to labor diligently in his business that his family may be as free as possible from financial worries.

The husband's spiritual ministry will include time each day for companionship with his wife. She desires some diversion from the domestic labors of the day and naturally she looks to her husband for this diversion. If she thinks of things for them to do together, he should agree enthusiastically and take part with her. But the husband will be at his best if he thinks of things to do together and then carries them through with real interest and relish. Frequently they should get away alone. A little trip or just a quiet walk in the park. All will be such a blessing to her as to minister to her happiness and her growth in grace.

III. The Instrument of the Husband's Ministry—"By the Word"

The instrument through which the husband is to accomplish his ministry of love is the Word, lived and taught. It is by the "washing of water by the word" (Eph. 5:26). The written Word is the instrument the Living Word (Christ) uses to perfect His Bride; and the husband as a co-worker with the Living Word has no other resource. It hardly needs to be said that every husband should "study to show himself approved, a workman that needeth not to be ashamed." If the husband is to fulfill his spiritual obligation to his wife, he must know the Word of God as thoroughly as he knows his trade; he must be as skillful in the handling of God's Word as he is in the handling of his business, or else he will be a failure as a husband.

The husband must "let the Word of Christ dwell in him," richly in all wisdom; teaching and admonishing his wife in Psalms and hymns and spiritual songs. (Col. 3:16). He must fill the life of his wife with spiritual sunshine; always have a word of encouragement for her from God's Word;

11

a counsel for her in a time of trial in her life; a choice morsel day by day to guide her growth and increase her strength in the things of the Lord. He must do all his work with the tenderness of Christ and a sweet spirit of humility.

IV. The Ground of the Husband's Ministry— "One Flesh"

Hodges says that the ground of the husband's spiritual ministry to his wife is "that unity that exists between man and wife." This unity is a unity of life made so by God. How husband and wife are united so as to form one life we do not fully understand, yet by revelation and experience we know husband and wife are "one flesh" (Gen. 2:24; Matt. 19:4-6). The truth of this statement can be seen again and again by anyone privileged to counsel with those in marital difficulties. How many times have we seen people who were divorced by the laws of man find that they were still attached to their mates in some inexplicable way! They couldn't break God's work of "one flesh" by a man-made rule. Only adultery severs that unity! Outside of adultery there is no power that can sever that unity. Many have utterly ruined their lives because they did not know or would not recognize this truth!

This intangible, indivisible unity of husband and wife is the ground of the husband's ministry. The wife, being united to him as intimately and really as his own body, may be loved as himself (Eph. 5:28, 29, 31). If the husband really understood the truth of one flesh, it would be as easy for him to love his wife as his own body, and as difficult for him to hate her as to hate his own body. He cannot harm her without harming himself. He cannot starve her spiritual life without starving himself. What he fails to do for her he fails to do for himself.

On Ephesians 5:29, Hodges observes: "Conjugal love

therefore, is as much a dictate of nature as self-love; and it is just as unnatural for a man to hate his wife as it would be for him to hate himself or his own body. A man may have a body which does not altogether suit him. He may wish it were handsomer, healthier, stronger, or more active. Still it is his body, it is himself; and he nourishes it and cherishes it tenderly as though it were the best and loveliest body man ever had. So a man may have a wife whom he could wish to be better, or more beautiful, or more agreeable; still she is his wife, and by the constitution of nature and ordinance of God—a part of himself. In neglecting her or ill using her he violates the laws of nature and the laws of God. It is thus Paul presents the matter. If the husband and wife are one flesh, the husband must love his wife, 'for no man ever yet hated his own flesh; but nourisheth and cherisheth it, even as the Lord the church.' "

The Greek for nourish means properly to nourish up, to train up by nurture, as a parent a child; the Greek for cherish means to warm, to cherish as a mother does an infant in her bosom. Both terms express tenderness and solicitude, and therefore both are suited to express the care with which every man provides for the wants and comforts of his own body. "Both terms express the heart and spirit of the husband's attitude, responsibility and ministry to his wife!"

The unity of husband and wife was made by God so that the husband would find it easier to carry out his obligation to his wife and more difficult to fail in it.

V. The Return of the Husband's Ministry—"He That Loveth His Wife Loveth Himself"

Because husand and wife are one flesh, all he does for his wife shall return in blessing upon himself. "He that loveth his wife loveth himself" (Eph. 5:28). The love poured into the life of the wife comes back again to him through her. If any husband complains that he receives little of spiritual blessing from his wife, he might seriously study to see if it is not also true that he gives very little to her.

The word husband means *house-band*. Thus husband is the one who binds the home together. One writer says: "Did you ever hear the word husband explained? It means literally the band of the house; the support of it, the person who keeps it together, as a band keeps together a sheaf of corn. There are many married men who are not husbands because they are not the band of the house." The husband is to band the marriage together by his ministry to the physical and spiritual needs of his wife.

If the husband does not operate effectively on both these levels, the band of that marriage is broken. When the band breaks, the spokes of the wheel fall apart; the bouquet of flowers fall scattered to the earth; the marriage may fall apart, and the lives of husband and wife be separated. God gave Adam a wife that she might be a help to him. The root meaning of the word help comes from a word meaning *a surrounder.* Thus the wife is one who surrounds her husband with love, sympathy, and tenderness. When the *band* of the husband is strong, then the two are bound together in a blessed unity of fellowship, and the wife is enabled to surround the husband with the return of all his blessings to her—pressed down and running over. Her full effectiveness as a surrounder depends on his effectiveness as a binder. It is interesting to know the meaning of the word wife; it means *weaver.* The husband in his spiritual ministry provides the wife with rich graces and blessings which she in turn weaves into the fabric of the marriage life to the joy and blessing of the whole family.

What the husband gives is not only given back to him, but pressed down and running over. Each seed of spiritual blessing he gives to his wife is multiplied and given back to him. When God took Eve from a part of Adam's body, Adam received that part in the multiplied form of hands that served him; eyes that looked upon him with interest; feet that followed him; a mind that thought with him; ears that heard him speak, a living body and soul that loved him. And God is still multiplying!

THE BRIDE'S PRAYER

Thou that the Author and the Giver art of all good things,
Without whose softening grace and ever present help,
The tenderest and best affections of the heart
     can yield no certain joy;
To Thee, O God, I turn e'en in the hour of solemn happiness,
Beseeching Thee, from Thy bright dwelling place,
The glad abode of peace on high, to look
Down on Thy trembling handmaid to grant that,
     as through new and untried scenes
I take my doubtful way and as fresh duties crowd
     across my path,
These weak and faltering steps
May be so guided by Thy gentle light
Which shineth only from above, that I
And my espoused fellow traveler with knitted hands
     and loving hearts may tread,
Unscathed life's rugged wild and reach at last,
The heavenly hills and everlasting rest,
The glorious purchase of the precious blood
That from His wounded side for sinners flowed
In whose great name, and for whose blessed sake
In humble trust, my bridal prayer I make.

Wife's Manual

15

2

THE CHRISTIAN WIFE
Proverbs 31:10-31

N THIS PORTION of God's Word, King Lemuel's mother
sets before him the full-length portrait of a virtuous
woman, the Christian wife, that choicest gift, which is said
to be "from the Lord" (Prov. 19:14). "It is an elegant poem
of twenty-two verses, like Psalm 119, constructed so that
each verse begins with one of the successive letters of the
Hebrew alphabet."

Bishop Horne in his sermon on "The Female Character"
said that all mothers and instructors should teach the female
pupils under their care to learn it by heart.

Matthew Henry says of this portion: "Thus is shut up
this looking-glass for ladies which they are desired to open
and dress themselves by; and if they do so, their adorning
will be found to praise and honor and glory at the appearing
of Jesus Christ."

Bishop Pilkington says, "If women would learn what God
will plague them for, and how; let them read the third
chapter of the prophet Isaiah. If they will learn what God
willeth them to do, and be occupied withal, though they be
of the best sort, let them read the last chapter of Proverbs. It
is enough to note it and point it out to them that will learn."

I. The Finding of a Virtuous Woman and Her Value

"Who can find a virtuous woman? for her price is far

above rubies." God would remind the young men that a Christian woman is priceless and is the only proper candidate for marriage to a young man who is looking for a treasure in a wife. "Who can find a virtuous woman?" A Christian wife is not to be gained by any haphazard methods. She must be sought, but not in one's own wisdom but in prayer, looking moment by moment to Him for guidance and counsel. The young man who seeks his wife by prayer, fully yielded to the mind of the Holy Spirit, will be guided to the virtuous woman who for him will have a price "far above rubies." For she will come not in her own name but in the name of Christ; not in her own will but in the will of Christ; in her hands she will bear precious treasures of graces and encouragements from the Father for the providential unfolding of his life's mission and work. Likewise, he then will come to her in the name and will of the Lord Jesus Christ bearing in his hands the graces and encouragements from the Father provided for the providential unfolding of her life's mission and work. Thus the answer to the vital question in verse ten throws us on the love, mercy, and guidance of God, and constrains us to look away from self and the energy of the flesh.

Bridges in his commentary on Proverbs 19:14 says: "The history of Ruth beautifully illustrates the train of matrimonial providence. The Moabitess married, contrary to all human probability, a man of Israel, that she might be brought into Naomi's family, return with her to her own land, and in the course of filial duty be brought under the eye and drawn to the heart of Boaz, her appointed husband (Ruth 1:1-4; 4:13). Often do the wheels of the Lord's working in this interesting matter constrain the admiration of men not well-exercised in spiritual observation (Gen. 24:50). And how much more endearing and secure is a special gift of God!" The Christian wife is a precious gift

of God, and aside from Christ she is the most precious gift
God ever gives to man! Oh! may we appreciate our Chris- ✓
tian wives as they ought to be appreciated!

It is also worthy of noting that God's question implies
that virtue is the only divinely recognized criterion for a
wife whose value is above rubies. We fear that too often
the search is made for beauty, accomplishment, personality,
glamour, or wealth, rather than solid virtue. Even Aris-
totle, the prince of Greek philosophy, said "If women be
good, the half of the commonwealth may be happy where
they are."

II. The Christian Wife Is a Fountain of Good to Her Husband

The heart of her husband doth safely trust in her, so that
he shall have no need of spoil. She will do him good and
not evil all the days of her life. The Christian wife is a
booster to her husband. She believes in him and she lets
him know she believes in him and in his future. All others
may look with indifference but as long as she encourages
him and believes in him, he will rise from strength to
strength.

Luther said of his wife, "The greatest gift of God is a
pious, amiable spouse, who fears God, loves His house, with
whom one can live in perfect confidence."

General Booth of the Salvation Army had such a wife.
"When the founder of the Salvation Army, the late General
Booth, was still in the Wesleyan ministry, a crisis arose.
He felt that God's call to him was to do the work of an
evangelist. But the Wesleyan Conference voted against his
giving his full time to this work. It was a crisis for William
Booth. If he refused to agree, then he would have to leave
the Wesleyan ministry. He and his family would lose their
income. His home and future would be threatened. One

18

can well understand the strongest of men hesitating. But while Mr. Booth was in the midst of the crisis, and as he was being urged to agree, a female voice was heard in the gallery shouting, 'William, never!' A woman had risen to her feet. A woman had dared to cry, 'Never!' It was Mrs. Booth. She with lionlike courage urged him to consequences with God. Instead of weeping and compromising because of difficulties that such a resignation would bring upon them, she was her husband's chief support. It was the beginning of the Salvation Army!"

No wonder at her funeral the sorrowing old General described her as "A tree who had shadowed him from the burning sun, whose flowers had been the adornment and beauty of his life, whose fruit had been the stay of his existence . . . a servant who had served without fee or reward . . . a counselor who had ever advised him, and seldom advised wrong . . . a friend who had understood his very nature . . . a wife who for forty years had never given him real cause for grief . . . who had ever been the strongest when the battle was strongest. She was the delight of his eyes and the inspiration of his soul. She was good—she was love—she was a spiritual warrior."

One may say that a Christian wife must be to her family what Shakespeare said sleep is to the body, "She must knit together the raveled sleeve of care. She is sore labors' bath balm of hurt minds, chief nourisher in life's feast. She is like a holy oil giving light and nourishment and warmth to those within her home, and to the wandering child she is 'like a candle that's set in a window at night.' "

III. The Christian Wife Is Called Blessed by Husband and Children

"Her children arise up, and call her blessed; her husband also, and he praiseth her" (Prov. 31:28). The Christian wife is loved and respected by her husband and children. This is so first of all because of what she is.

1. Virtuous (v. 10)
2. A fountain of good (v. 12)
3. A willing worker (v. 13)
4. Self-sacrificing for her family (vv. 14, 15)
5. Financially careful, systematic, and wise. She considers budgets and saves her husband's money (v. 16).
6. She is strong to labor for the good of her family, rearing her children, caring for the sick, and doing all the other numberless duties wives attend to in the home. (v. 17).
7. She is a tireless worker for the well-being of her loved ones. It is true that "woman's work is never done" (v. 18).
8. She is kind to the poor (v. 20).
9. She provides for the needs of her family (v. 21).
10. She is well-groomed (v. 22).
11. Because of her life, her husband is honored and respected among the men of the town, in business, etc. (v. 23).
12. She is strong in character and honorable in all her relationships (v. 25).
14. She is a wise counselor and very kind. Her tongue is sweet and kind (v. 26), and with the wisdom of her lips she feeds the souls of her loved ones.
14. She is not lazy or idle (v. 27).
15. She fears the Lord. She loves God, and her love for Him furnishes the motive power for all her deeds, thoughts and desires. (v. 30).

Is it any wonder that her children call her blessed and that her husband praises her? This is the fruit of her hands, and her praise is the testimony of her works.

Perhaps one especially characteristic mark of the Christian

wife is the burden and interest she bears on her heart for the spiritual welfare of her family. How many men will arise on the Great Day and before all assembled creation give thanks to God for their faithful wives who prayed and loved them into the heart of Christ! How many sons and how many daughters will throughout the endless ages call mother "blessed" because she loved and prayed them into the heart of Christ! Dwight L. Moody in his Chicago meeting of October, 1876, gave the following illustrations to encourage Christian wives and mothers to pray for the salvation of their loved ones:

"I remember at one of the meetings at Nashville during the war a young man came to me, trembling from head to foot. 'What is the trouble?' I asked. 'There is a letter I got from my sister, and she tells me every night as the sun goes down she goes on her knees and prays for me.' This man was brave, and had been in a number of battles; he could stand before the cannon's mouth, yet this letter completely upset him. 'I have been trembling ever since I received it.' Six hundred miles away the faith of this girl went to work, and its influence was felt by the brother. He did not believe in prayer; he did not believe in Christianity; he did not believe in his mother's Bible. This mother was a praying woman, and when she died she left on earth a praying daughter. And when God saw her faith and heard that prayer, He answered her. How many sons and daughters could be saved if their mothers and fathers but had faith!

"At Murfeesboro another illustration of this occurred. A young man received a letter from his mother in which she said something life this: 'My Dear Boy: You do not know how I am burdened for your salvation! Every morning and evening I go into my closet and pray for you, that you may be led to the cross of Christ. You may die in battle, or in the hospitals, and oh, my son, I want you to become a

Christian. I do not know but that this will be my last letter to you.' This young lieutenant come to me and said, 'I have just heard of my mother's death, and I have prayed for forgiveness of my sins.' He was converted just through his mother's faith. Although she was in glory, her voice was heard here.

"In one of the towns in England there is a beautiful little chapel, and a very touching story is told in connection with it. It was built by an infidel. He had a praying wife, but he would not listen to her, would not allow her pastor even to take dinner with them, would not look at the Bible, would not allow religion ever to be talked of. She made up her mind, seeing she could not influence him by her voice, that every day she would pray to God at twelve o'clock for his salvation. She said nothing to him, but every day at that hour she told the Lord about her husband. At the end of twelve months there was no change in him.

"But she did not give up; six months more went by. Her faith began to waver and she said, 'Will I have to give him up at last? Perhaps when I am dead, He will answer my prayers.' When she got to that point it seemed just as if God had got her where He wanted her. The man came home to dinner one day. His wife was in the dining room waiting for him, but he didn't come in. She waited for some time and finally looked for him all through the house. At last she thought of going into that little room where she had prayed so often. There he was, praying with agony where she had prayed for so many months, asking forgiveness for his sins. And this is the lesson to you wives who have infidel husbands. The Lord saw that woman's faith and answered her prayer.

"We cannot but think of that consecrated wife whom we had the joy of learning about in a little parish in the southern part of the state. Her husband was unsaved, and he had a brutal, aggressive hatred for the things of God. But this Christian wife had a burning passion for his salvation, and her burning passion issued forth in pleading and persevering prayer. She recounts: 'Many a time when I was praying for him with tear-blinded eyes he would slip into the room and pour a bucketful of water over me. He would taunt me and jest at me with fiendish hatred.

" 'But I kept on praying and would permit nothing to turn me from this holy exercise. And I prayed God to give me the grace of sweetness that I might never become revengeful or vindictive. God answered prayer first in me. He gave me grace to pray on year in and year out with no discouragement or doubt that my husband would be saved, and He gave me the grace to keep sweet and return good for evil, that my prayers be not hindered by my life. After many years of heartache, pleading prayers, cruel insults, and fiendish persecution, he utterly broke down and cried to the Lord for mercy.' This man later testified that the constant praying and loving sweetness of his wife under the most bitter pressures year in and year out caused him, by God's grace, to know the reality of Christ. 'I couldn't deny the Christ I saw in her.' If there is anyone with an unsaved loved one, take courage—pray on and keep sweet, and God will win that lost loved one's soul to Himself. We can say with great confidence that no one will ever see the fires of hell if he has only one Christian who will pray for his salvation."

IV. The Christian Wife Is a Counselor with Wisdom and Kindness

"She openeth her mouth with wisdom; and in her tongue is the law of kindness" (Prov. 31:26). The Christian wife is sometimes an unacclaimed expert in personal counseling. She may never have taken a course in psychology or pastoral theology and she may know little or nothing about psychiatry; probably she will never be rewarded with an honorary doctorate. She may not know anything about the theory of counseling, but she knows how to practice it. She knows God and loves Him. She studies His Word and she spends time alone each day in communion with Him. Like Abraham, she becomes a friend of God and like Enoch she walks with God. Thus does she learn the ways of God and this is the source of her wisdom. A minister greatly used of God testified: "Sometimes the weight, care and problems of life weigh upon the mind, and all seems darkness. We question and wonder just what the answer could be. We cry to God for light and then, for me anyway, He sends me to my wife. When the problem is laid out before her she knows just what to say to flood light into my mind. Just a little talk with her and my mind is clear and my heart is filled with fresh confidence and renewed courage; the mist has cleared and the vision is clear again before my eyes."

Another Christian man, a businessman with responsibilities that claim the utmost resources of the mind and body said: "My hours are irregular, but no matter what time I get home I must have a talk with my wife. She is always radiant and she is always the same. I share the joys and victories of the day with her. And she always has something to say that multiplies the joys and makes the victories more precious. And then if there have been any, I must share the griefs and disappointments with her. She always understands. It may be that something she was reading from the Bible that very day will have a special bearing on my problem. She will tell me about it and in a little while as she shares her love, faith and understanding with me, my anxiety and fear and worry are all gone. I often tell her she is my chief consultant." God says of the virtuous woman that, "She openeth her mouth with wisdom."

One of the greatest powers of the personal counselor, according to authorities, is love. Love enables the counselor to put himself in the place of the other person. One distraught, nervous patient has been conferring with a professional counselor and has been much encouraged. She may not remember all the ideas the counselor gives her; but one thing he has said stands out in her mind and has made a deep impression on her: "Remember we are in this thing together." The statement reveals a concern that has caused the counselor to put himself in this patient's place, and the patient has sensed the power of this creative sympathy and has responded with fresh courage.

But who can practice the noble art of putting oneself in the place of another as the virtuous Christian wife? In this art she excels all others. From her Saviour she has learned the art of sharing the lives of others. Many times she says little, but at such times her silence is the sympathizing silence of real compassion. And this silence of which she is such a master is revealing of a Third whose recognized Presence is the sufficient answer to every need of the moment!

"For where two or three are gathered together in my name, there am I in the midst of them." She knows Him, and knowing Him she knows how to fill her silences with Christ and thus with healing and light.

God says that in her tongue is the law of kindness. When she speaks, her words are full of kindly consideration and Christly compassion. With her kindness she feeds the heart-need for understanding and for love. One such wife in a time of her husband's deep perplexity wrote the following little note to her husband:

Why should I shrink from poverty
  If it be shared, dear love, with thee?
The world's neglect, the proud one's scorn,

How easily can they be borne
Whilst thou remainest unforsworn and true to me!
I little reck that with our name
   The crowd may pity join, or blame;
That fickle ones, whom once we ranged
   Amongst our friends, are now estranged;
For thou, art thou not all unchanged, and still the same?
Though to our board no menial train
   Shall bear the plenteous feast again,
With willing hand will I prepare
   The frugal meal thou art to share,
And joy to find my housewife care is not in vain;
And loving voices shall be here
   With social mirth thy breast to cheer;
And sounds of household minstrelsy
   The hymn, the song, the well-known glee
How often shall they win from thee no bitter tear!

Wife's Manual

Perhaps it would be impossible to better demonstrate the
value of a loving wife and the sanctuary of home which
her love makes than by reference to Cowper. No one could
have written "The Task" whose heart was not warm with
the joy of a Christian wife's love and of consoling domestic
scenes. Cowper was, to an unusual degree, a man of des-
pondency and sorrow. His mental sufferings were most
acute. Every fiber of his poet's soul seemed to shrink from
contact with the world. It was the fireside which afforded
the only retreat he could find to soothe his feelings. He found
comfort in his wife and in their home. As soon as he was
out in the crude world, the gloom settled deep and heavy
on his mind. His delicate feelings could not endure contact
with earth's cold blasts. Had it not been for the soothing
influence of his wife's love and his happy home, Cowper

would never have escaped being a frantic inmate in the mental hospital.

What an insight does Cowper give us to his own heart, as he says; " 'Tis pleasant through the loopholes of retreat, to peep at such a world; to see the stir of the great Babel, and not feel the crowd; to hear the roar she sends through all her gates at a safe distance, where the dying sounds, falls a soft murmur on the uninjured." Behind those words is the joy and blessing of a good wife and the sanctuary of home she made for him away from the storms of life.

Mrs. J. Hudson Taylor, in a letter written to her husband on November 10, 1873, beautifully exemplifies the wisdom and kindness that belongs to the Christian wife. "I feel, darling, that we must lean fully and constantly on Jesus if we are to get on at all, and I have been seeking to do it, and in believing prayer to bring our many needs to Him. I have written down the names of our foreign and native helpers, that I may be able to plead for them all daily. If we would have power for what Jesus calls us to do, we must not expend it in bearing burdens that He would have us cast on Him, must we? And there is abundant supply with Him for all this work, for all we need, isn't there? It's unbelief that saps our strength and makes everything look dark; and yet He reigns, and we are one with Him, and He is making everything happen for the very best: and so we ought always to rejoice in Him, and rest, though it is not always easy. We must triumph with God, and then we shall succeed with men, and be made blessings to them. You know these things, and can put them much better than I can; but still it does us good to remind one another, doesn't it?"

V. The Christian Wife Fears the Lord

"Favor is deceitful, and beauty is vain: but a woman

that feareth the Lord, she shall be praised" (Prov. 31:30). Here is the heart of this grand portrait of a virtuous woman and precious wife. Here is the motivation for her deeds of mercy; the fountainhead of all her domestic praise; the quickening power for her ambition and moderation. Here is the source of her strength, wisdom and kindness that makes her a counselor. Her fear is not a slavish fear but is based on her love of God. She fears to displease Him because she loves Him so much. She fears to do or say anything that would bring grief to His heart or dishonor to His holy name. She would rather have sorrow with God than the world's joy without God, for she knows that sorrow with God is blessed and joy of pleasure without God is cursed. She has learned from God that beauty without Him is vain and a snare, and favor without Him is deceitful. With the Psalmist she could exclaim, "The Lord is my portion . . . I will bless the Lord at all times: his praise shall continually be in my mouth. My soul shall make her boast in the Lord! the humble shall hear thereof and be glad. O magnify the Lord with me, and let us exalt his name together" (Ps. 34:1-3). Her counsel is wise, for "the secret of the Lord is with them that fear him; and he will show them his covenant" (Ps. 25:14). In her life she daily demonstrates the truth of God's Word: "The meek will he guide in judgment: and the meek will he teach his way."

Her reverence and love for God is the motivating center for all her work. Whether it is the routine duties of everyday housework, such as washing wishes, dusting the furniture, baking a cake or washing clothes, she escapes the dullness of these routine jobs for she obeys Colossians 3:17: "And whatsoever ye do in word or deed, do all in the name of the Lord Jesus, giving thanks to God and the Father by him." Because she does everything for Him, it is ever a delight and always a blessing. This is what Brother Lawrence called "practicing the presence of God." He worked each day in the kitchen in the name of Christ and for the glory of Christ, and found in that kitchen a "little bit of heaven to go to heaven in." When Brother Lawrence began his business of the day he said to God, with a childlike trust in Him: "O my God, since Thou art with me and I must now, in obedience to Thy commands, apply my mind to these outward things, I beseech Thee to grant me the grace to continue in Thy presence; and to this end do Thou prosper me with Thine assistance, receive all my works, and possess all my affections."

Brother Lawrence testified, "We can do little things for God. I turn the cake that is frying on the pan for love of Him, and that done, if there is nothing else to call me, I prostrate myself in worship before Him, who has given me grace to work; afterwards I rise happier than a king. It is enough for me to pick up but a straw from the ground for the love of God."

Jeremy Taylor gives five sure results of thus practicing the presence of God.

1. It is an excellent help to prayer, producing in us a deep reverence for the majesty of God.
2. It produces a confidence in God; a fearlessness of our enemies; patience in trouble and a sure hope of remedy.
3. It produces joy in God, for we know He is with us in our natural actions to preserve us; in our public actions to applaud or reprove us; in our recreations to restrain us; in our sleep to watch by us, and in our watchings to refresh us. Realizing all this, it is easy to keep Paul's rule to "rejoice in the Lord alway."
4. It enkindles holy desires of the enjoyment of God.
5. It issues forth as a fountain of humility of spirit; apprehensions of our great needs; our daily wants and

hourly supplies; deep admiration of God's unspeakable mercies. It helps to recollection of mind and restrains the scatterings and looseness of wandering thoughts. It is a great cause of moderation in our actions.

WORDS OF WIFE TO HUSBAND
OR
HOME CHARMS

Wouldst thou have our own dear dwelling
   Be a love-enchanted home?
Spells I'll try, and there's no telling
   How much so it may become.
Sunny smiles around I'll scatter,
   Brightest still when thou art near;
Use fond words, but never flatter,
   Smiles and words alike sincere.
Round my heart I will assemble
   Things and thoughts, beloved, of thee,
Till each wish and taste resemble
   Those that in thy bosom be;
As the maid at midnight hour
   Ever watched, so legends say,
The beacon fire upon her tower
   To guide her lover's lonely way.
When the world shall wrong or slight thee,
   Midst thy bosom's bitter pain
The warmth of home shall lure and light thee,
   To my welcome clasp again.
Then with fond words and caresses
   Shalt thou by our fireside's blaze
Tell how all the day's distresses
   One such evening hour repays.

               Wife's Manual

3

THE CHRISTIAN WIFE'S
RESPONSIBILITY OF SUBJECTION

*Wives, submit yourselves unto your own husbands, as
unto the Lord. For the husband is the head of the wife, even
as Christ is the head of the church: and he is the saviour of
the body. Therefore as the church is subject unto Christ, so
let the wives be to their own husbands in everything. Husbands, love your wives, even as Christ also loved the church,
and gave himself for it. Nevertheless let every one you in
particular so love his wife even as himself; and the wife see
that she reverence her husband.*

—Ephesians 5:22-25, 33

IN THIS COMMANDMENT we have the divine key to any
woman's being a happy, faithful, and successful wife. In
the portion before us the apostle teaches the nature, ground,
and extent of the obedience due from the wife to the husband.

As to the nature of it, it is spiritual; it is as to the Lord.
The obedience of the wife to the husband is to be regarded
as part of her obedience to the Lord. As Hodges says, "It
terminates on Him, and therefore is religious, because determined by religious motives and directed towards the object of the religious affections." Here explains and answers
the chief difficulty in the thinking of most people, even believers, regarding this basic marital commandment. All too
many consider the commandment as teaching obedience to

here

the husband. When this is the understanding it naturally ministers to the pride of man and the inferiority of woman. The true teaching places the whole subject in an entirely different perspective. The obedience is to the Lord and through the husband. That is, the wife is commanded to obey Christ through her obedience to her husband. Thus the obedience is spiritual in motive and religious in objective. Christ is the motive and the objective of her obedience to her husband.

The ground of the obedience is not only in commandment but also in nature. Hodges says, "The Apostle says wives are to be obedient to their husbands, because the husband is the head of the wife, even as Christ is the Head of the church. The ground of the obligation, therefore as it exists in nature, is the eminency of the husband, his superiority in those attributes which enable and entitle him to command. He is larger, stronger, bolder; has more of those mental and moral qualities which are required in a leader. This is just as plain from history as that iron is heavier than water. The man, therefore, in this aspect, is qualified and entitled to command, is said to be the image and glory of God (I Cor. 11:17); for, as the Apostle adds in that connection, the man was not made out of the woman, but the woman out of the man; neither was the man created for the woman; but the woman for the man. This superiority of the man (by divine decree—thus removing any basis for boasting in man) in the respects mentioned, thus taught in Scripture, founded in nature, and proved by all experience, cannot be denied or disregarded without destroying society and degrading both men and women; making the one effeminate and the other masculine."

Shakespeare saw the truth and importance of man's lordship and woman's subjection to his rule and authority:

"Katharina, one of Shakespeare's great characters in *The*

Taming of the Shrew, shows a deep understanding of man's and woman's natures, and their different roles in married life. When two women scorned and defied their husbands, she beautifully explained to them the love and respect a woman owes her husband.

Fie, fie! unknit that threatening, unkind brow;
And dart not scornful glances from those eyes
To wound thy lord, thy king, thy governor.
It blots thy beauty, as frosts do bite the meads;
Confounds thy fame, as whirlwinds shade fair buds;
And in no sense is meet or amiable.
A woman moved is like a fountain troubled,
Muddy, ill-seeming, thick, bereft of beauty;
And, while it is so, none so dry or thirsty
Will deign to sip, or touch one drop of it.
Thy husband is thy lord, thy life, thy keeper,
Thy head, thy sovereign; one that cares for thee,
And for thy maintenance! Commits his body
To painful labor, both by sea and land;
To watch the night in storms, the day in cold,
While thou liest warm at home, secure and safe,
And craves no other tribute at thy hands,
But love, fair looks, and true obedience,—
Too little payment for so great a debt.
Such duty as the subject owes the prince
Even such a woman owes to her husbnd;
And when she's froward, peevish, sullen, **sour,**
And not obedient to his honest will,
What is she, but a foul, contending rebel
And graceless traitor to her loving lord?
I am ashamed that women are so simple
To offer war where they should kneel for **peace;**
Or seek for rule, supremacy, and sway,
When they are bound to serve, love and obey.

> Why are our bodies soft, and weak, and smooth,
> Unapt to toil and trouble in the world,
> But that our soft conditions and our hearts
> Should well agree with our external parts?

We like the fine, clear, statement of the great commentator Eadie on this point: "As Christ is Head of the Church, so the husband is head of the wife. Authority and government are lodged in him; the household has its unity and centre in him; from him the wife receives her cherished help; his views and feelings are naturally adopted and acted out by her; and to him she looks up for instruction and defense. Severed from him she becomes a widow, desolate and cheerless; the ivy which clasped itself so lovingly round the oak, pines and withers when the tree has fallen, and there is only one head; dualism would be perpetual antagonism. This marital headship is man's prerogative in virtue of his prior creation, for he was first formed in sole and original dignity (I Tim. 2:13). Man was not created for the woman, but the woman for the man, and he is in *position superior* (I Cor. 11:9). 'The man is not of the woman, but the woman of the man.' A portion of himself—his other self; taken out from near his heart and therefore—though his equal in personality and fellowship—being of him and for him and after him, she is still second to him. That is, in authority and government. Nay, more, 'Adam was not deceived: but the woman, being deceived, was in the transgression'; and to her the Lord God said, 'Thy desire shall be to thy husband, and he shall rule over thee,' though the gospel lightens this position of the curse which has been so terribly felt in all non-Christians lands each sex is indeed imperfect by itself, and the truest unity is in conjugal duality (I Cor. 11:11). Still, though the woman was originally of the man, yet now 'the man is by the woman,' 'the mother of all living.' Finally, the Apostle illustrates this

34

headship by the beautiful sentiment, that the woman is the 'glory of the man,' but 'the man is the image and glory of God' (I Cor. 11:7)." Eadie says, in part, on Ephesians 5:25: "The submission of the wife is in kind that of the Church to Christ. It is not forced, but it springs from loyal attachment, from her conscious need of support and protection, from a just view of the relationship in which she stands as a helpmate, and of the original and continued destiny of her sex. She may be in other things man's superior— in delicacy of sentiment, warmth of devotion, strength of moral heroism, power and patience of self-denial, and general sympathy with suffering and distress. Still the obedience inculcated by the Apostle sits gracefully upon her, and is in harmony with all that is fair and feminine, in her position and temperament.

"For contemplation he and valour formed—
For softness she and sweet attractive grace,
He for God only, she for God and him."

On Ephesians 5:33, Eadie says: "One peculiarity in this injunction has been usually overlooked. What is instinctive on either side is not enforced, but what is necessary to direct and hallow such an instinct is inculcated. The woman loves in deep, undying sympathy; but to teach her how this fondness should know and fill its appropriate sphere, she is commanded to obey and honor. The man, on the other hand, feels that his position is to govern; but to show him what should be the essence and means of his government, he is enjoined to love. When this balance of power is unsettled, happiness is lost, and mutual recriminations ensue."

Jeremy Taylor in his Sermon on the Marriage Ring (*Works*, Vol. 15) says, "He rules her by authority, and she rules him by love; she ought by all means to please him, and he must by no means displease her."

"A masterly wife," Gattaker says, "is as much despised and derided for taking rule over her husband as he for yielding to it."

Ephesians 5:22 teaches the extent of the wife's subjection to her husband. She is to be subject to him in everything. This does not mean that the authority of the husband is unlimited, but rather it teaches its extent and not its degree. "It extends," as Hodges wisely says, "over all departments but is limited in all; first, by the nature of the relation; and secondly, by the higher authority of God. No superior, whether master, parent, husband or magistrate, can make it obligatory on us either to do what God forbids, or not to do what God commands. So long as our allegiance to God is preserved, and obedience to man is made part of our obedience to him, we retain our liberty and our integrity."

Nowhere is the great power of such subjection more clearly brought to our attention than in I Peter 3:1-6. Note that verse 1 begins with subjection and ends with power. In verse four God puts His evaluation on woman's lowly subjection as "of great price."

Augustine in Book 9 of his Confessions provides what might be aptly termed a rich and fitting commentary on I Peter 3:1-6. He says of his mother: "Brought up thus modestly and soberly, and made subject by Thee to her parents, then by her parents to Thee, so soon as she was of marriageable age, being given to a husband, she served him as her lord; and did her diligence to win him unto Thee, preaching Thee unto him by her conversation; by which Thou didst ornament her, making her reverently lovable, and admirable to her husband, and she so endured the wronging of her bed as never to have any quarrel with her husband thereon. For she looked for Thy mercy upon him, that believing in Thee, he might be made chaste. But besides this, he was fervid, as in his affections, so in anger; but she

36

had learnt not to resist an angry husband, not in deed only, nor even in word. Only when he was smoothed and tranquil and in a temper to receive it, she would give an account of her actions, if perchance he had overhastily taken offence. *In a word, while many matrons, who had milder husbands, yet bore even in their faces marks of shame, would in a familiar talk blame their husbands' lives,* she would blame their tongues, giving them, as in jest, earnest advice; 'That from the time they heard the marriage writings read to them, they should account them as indentures whereby they were made servants; and so, remembering their condition, ought not to set themselves up against their lords.' And when they, knowing what a choleric husband she endured, marvelled that it had never been heard, nor by any token perceived, that Patricius had beaten his wife, or that there had been any domestic difference between them, even for one day, and confidentially asking the reason, she taught them her practice above mentioned. Those wives who observd it found the good, and returned thanks; those who observed it not found no relief, and suffered."

After two paragraphs of praise for the sweet meekness of his mother, Augustine goes on to say, "Finally, her own husband, towards the very end of his earthly life, did she gain unto Thee; nor had she to complain of that in him as a believer, which before he was a believer she had borne from him. She was also the servant of Thy servants; whosoever of them knew her, did in her much praise and honour and love Thee; for that through the witness of the fruits of a holy conversation they perceived Thy presense in her heart. For she had been the wife of a man, had requited her parents, had governed her house piously, was well reported of for good works, had brought up children, so often travailing in birth of them as she saw them swerving from God."

CHRISTIAN'S CLOCK

And Christian made a shrine for the hours the Lord had given him; and from the shrine a golden chain was linked to the great bell at the prayer-gate, and when the bell struck, the angel opened the gate and gave back the answer.

—Bunyan's *Pilgrim's Progress.*

The bell tolls one—
Teach me to say,
"Thy will be done."

The bell tolls two—
Help me each day
Thy will to do.

The bell tolls three—
I ask in faith
To follow Thee.

The bell tolls four—
I pray for trust
Forevermore.

The bell tolls five
For Christian speech
Help me to strive.

The bell tolls six—
Teach me my hope
On Thee to fix.

The bell tolls seven—
Oh, make my life
A way to heaven.

The bell tolls eight—
   May I in peace
And patience wait.

The bell tolls nine—
   Let Charity
Be ever mine.

The bell tolls ten—
   I pray for love
To God and men.

It tolls eleven—
   Let me each hour
Be nearer heaven.

Twelve strokes I hear!
   Now perfect love
Hath cast out fear.

4

PRACTICAL COUNSELS OF CHRISTIAN MARRIAGE

I Corinthians 13; Colossians 3:12-25; Ephesians 4:17-32; Matthew 5:1-16

I. Recognize Basic Differences

REMEMBER THE DIFFERENCE between the sexes. Man is man, woman is woman. There are basic and fundamental differences in their makeup, their personalities and outlook on life.

The man usually approaches life from the level of cold reason, whereas woman lives more in her affections and emotions. Failure to understand this basic difference is responsible for much tension and friction in households. The chief temptation of the man is to become bitter at the woman because of her way of reasoning and her approach to life. That is why God has especially commanded, "Husbands love your wives, and be not bitter against them" (Col. 3:19). The tendency is so deep and the temptation so strong that God has again commanded it in I Peter 3:7.

It is always well to remember that reason without emotion would be cold, hard, and lifeless; and emotion without reason would be unguided, unprofitable, and destructive. Thus husband and wife complement each other and become instruments of growth and grace to each other. The woman is tempted to become provoked at her husband's cold, rational approach to life, and that is why God has especially commanded her in Ephesians 5:33, "And the wife see that she reverence her husband." Bitterness and irreverence are the two basic temptations to husband and wife respectively— basic because they have reference to the basic differences of the masculine and feminine personalities. Husband and wife should be diligently on the lookout and should make it a matter of persevering prayer that they may not enter into temptation.

II. Don't Live with Parents

In ancient times, parents gave a dowry to their daughter when she married. The express purpose of the dowry was that the young married couple might have sufficient resources to set up a home of their own. It might be wise to restore this custom. Friction is sure to develop if a young couple attempts to live under a parent's roof. The adjustments and problems of two young lives seeking to live and grow together are great enough without adding more. Jesus said, "A man will leave his father and mother and cleave to his wife."

Christ demands this separation from parents at the time of marriage. Those who refuse to obey this divine commandment and allow themselves to remain with their parents "just for a few months until we can get on our feet," live to regret this disobedience. Begin marriage away from parents in your own room or apartment just with each other and Jesus!

III. Give and Receive Admonition

When we think there is a real fault in our loved one, what shall we do? Shall we immediately decide upon admonishing the offending member? No, we think it is much the better part of wisdom to walk softly and carefully seek to know the mind of the Lord.

We should pray first. We should pray for our offending

loved one. It is remarkable how a personality will change under the quickening power of someone's prevailing prayer of faith. An elderly man after being saved prayed for his wife who was subject to spells of jealousy. As he prayed for her in the quiet of his closet he discovered two things: (1) He found himself able to keep sweetly quiet while she spent the fury of her jealousy in many harsh words. We cannot speak harsh words to one for whom we are praying. (2) Secondly, after he had prayed for his wife for many weeks, he found her spells of jealousy lessening in intensity, duration and frequency. Finally they ceased altogether. Under the blessing of his daily loving prayer for his wife, her life was beautifully changed. Prayer for our loved one opens that life to the ministry of the Holy Spirit. As we continue praying, He continues working upon that life until the complete victory is won.

Then we must seek for understanding of our loved one's faults. Frequently the cause of a fault needs changing rather than the person.

Many a person's disagreeable ways rest upon causes that are hidden even from the offender himself. Such causes may be: (1) wounded pride; (2) a lurking sense of inadequacy and inferiority; (3) a deep sense of fear; (4) physical fatigue and run-down condition; (5) a deep sorrow that may have turned to bitterness through the years; (6) loneliness. If any of these reasons are behind the faults of your loved one, pray accordingly and do whatever else you find possible to relieve the condition. Above all, show love and understanding, for love never faileth.

If, after much prayer and study one feels it wise to speak a word of counsel to the loved one, let it be in the spirit of I Corinthians 13 and Galatians 6:1-3. We believe the counsel of Pastor Byfield on the giving and receiving of admonition will be helpful at this point.

"In performing admonition we must especially look to two things: First, that the ground of admonition be out of the Word of God, being the words of Christ, not our own words. To this end we should store ourselves and hold fast the faithful word according to doctrine. Secondly, we must see that the manner of admonition be right. Admonition is to be performed: First, with *innocency*; we must not be faulty ourselves, or if we have been we must plainly acknowledge it before we admonish. Second, with *discretion*, which must be shown in two things:

"(a) That we are sure that they have offended; not led to it by the suspicion of our own hearts or by hearsay or by outward appearance, but judge by the hearing of our ears and the sight of our eyes.

"(b) We must know it to be an offense; we must consider whether it be of the number of those offenses a wise man must hold his glory to pass by (Prov. 19:11).

"Third, it must be done seasonably, with love, admonishing as a brother (II Thess. 3:5); fourth, with *meekness* (Gal. 6:1); fifth, with secrecy (Matt. 18:15; Prov. 25:9); sixth with plainness—spare no words to satisfy them (Lev. 19:17); seventh, with compassion and tenderness (II Cor. 2:4); eighth, with perseverance, we must not be weary and discouraged, but accomplish it (Prov. 13:19); ninthly, with all authority (Titus 2:1) that neither ourselves nor God's ordinances be defiled.

"In receiving admonition we must

"(a) Receive it with love and self-examination (I Thess. 5:12).

"(b) With all humility, readily inclined to suspect ourselves, knowing we have cause to say and think of ourselves as that worthy man did, 'I am more brutish than any man, and have not the understanding of a man' (Prov. 30:2; I Thess. 5:12; Prov. 30:2, 3).

"(c) With subjection and direct acknowledgment, giving glory to God.

"(d) With reformation, else all is in vain."

IV. Accept Each Other

Husband and wife must accept each other as they are in the present, with all their virtues and faults. Every human being is faulty and frail. One of the great purposes of marriage is growth. Each is to be a means of grace, encouragement and help to the other that both may grow in the likeness and image of Christ. The apostle Paul sets forth the true spirit and attitude of marriage in II Timothy 2:24-26 and Colossians 3:12-17. You will notice the passage in Colossians directly precedes Paul's statement addressed to wives, husbands, children, and fathers. This whole passage is to be the spirit and attitude of each member of the family toward the other. With this deep, rich, spiritual attitude prevailing, all are accepted as they are that they might grow to be more like Him in thought, word and deed. Every husband and wife should read, memorize, pray over and meditate upon Colossians 3:12-17 with such frequency that it's spirit will be their spirit toward each other. This is truly the spirit of each for all and all for each.

V. Do Not Talk about or Reveal Faults and Sins of the Past

(Rom. 7:18; Gal. 5:17-26). Only a misguided sense of loyalty would cause wife or husband to reveal faults and sins of the past at the feet of a loved one. God's Word is clear that we are to forget "those things which are behind, and reach forth unto those things which are before" (see Phil. 3:12-15).

True love should be above all such unwise curiosity about the past. If two people truly love each other, they should take each other for what they are now. The past should be forgiven and forgotten automatically. True love and true Christian faith rise above all suspicions of the past, and see others as they are before God in the cleansing blood of Christ—clean, justified, accepted in the Beloved. Let us ever keep our eyes on what we *are* in Christ (I John 3:1-3; Col. 2:9; 1:21) and where we are in Christ (Col. 2:11-15; Eph. 2:13-22). Instead of husband and wife dwelling on the possible mistakes, sins and shortcomings of the past, let them rather pray that God will show them what they are today, being in Christ. Let them pray with Paul that great prayer in Ephesians 3:14-21. What manner of persons we are in Christ! We should never be desirous of returning to the flesh pots of Egypt in memory or conversation, for that would surely grieve the Holy Spirit (see Eph. 4:29, 30) and fill the life with bitterness (Eph. 4:31). It is wise to forget the past and let the attitude be as the Holy Spirit has commanded; "And be ye kind one to another, tenderhearted, forgiving one another, even as God for Christ's sake hath forgiven you" (Eph. 4:32).

VI. Don't Tattle Family Secrets

Guard your loved one's reputation with all diligence and hide every fault away in your heart and at the throne of grace. Somehow your loved one will sense your faithfulness and will trust you with unwavering confidence. And this is the very cornerstone of love.

Miriam's sin was that of gossip. Miriam professed to be offended with Zipporah, the Ethiopian wife of Moses. The Lord saw it and rebuked her, saying, "Wherefore were ye not afraid to speak against Moses?" God says people should be afraid to speak against another in private and behind his back. Why? Because God sees it and will judge it. He smote Miriam with leprosy—until, utterly

45

humiliated and deeply humbled, she repented. God healed her after she had repented.

Let there be no Miriams in our households. Let not the in-laws nor any of the relatives be like Miriam in respect to criticism.

R. E. Baldwin says: "Full well I know that but few intend to be guilty of the sin of detraction—Miriam's sin. I know with many it is the result of thoughtlessness; but its influence extends much farther than they ever imagine; it excites prejudices in the young who hear it, which will live long after those who uttered it are dead; it wrings many innocent hearts, and they and God only know the bitter tears that are shed on account of it."

Full oft a word that lightly leaves the tongue,
Another heart unnecessarily has wrung;
And were the wound but present to the eye,
We'd mourn the pain that solace might defy.

Was it a taunt, perhaps a thoughtless jest,
An idle ripple on the vacant breast?
But thy shafts may yield a venomed death—
What need to speed them but a little breath!

We toy with hearts as if the thousand chords,
That vibrate to the touch of hasty words,
Could join our discords all the livelong day,
Nor any tension cause them to give way.

Oh, strike them gently; every human breast
Is by a secret load of grief opprest;
Forbear to add a note of timeless woe
Where discords ever are so prone to flow.

Author Unknown

Spurgeon said, "Love stands in the presence of a fault with finger on her lips."

If you must share your burden with someone, go to your pastor whom you may rest assured will give you wise counsel. We are anxious to see the day return when the pastor will again be sought out as the counselor of troubled souls. Now, in all too many cases, counseling is a minor part of the pastor's ministry. Yet the need today for this type of ministry is greater than ever.

VII. Don't Shower All Your Affection on Your Child

The new baby brings new joy, but sometimes because of a foolish, selfish mother, his coming introduces tension and unhappiness in the home. It is a great temptation for this new life to become the all-absorbing object of the mother's attention until the husband feels himself all but forgotten. Such fastening of a mother's love on her new baby may dim her love for her husand. Let the new mother be careful to bring her child into her love for her husband. It was this deep, shared love between husband and wife that gave the little one life and brought him into the world. It is in this *shared love* that he will grow to emotional and spiritual maturity. If the wife breaks this precious fellowship and sets the child up as the complete object of her love and attention (even though done unintentionally), an unnatural situation develops which is full of serious consequences for husband, wife, and child. The emotional and spiritual satisfaction of each member of the family depends on their shared love. In the case of the mother doting upon the child, the father is denied the wife's love, and the child is denied some of his father's love; it makes an emotional widow out of the mother for she has cut herself free from her husband's love and affection. The child grows into adulthood an emotional misfit, with a deep sense of insecurity.

"In connection with Charles M. Alexander's marriage to Miss Cadbury, he gave her a ring inscribed with words: 'Each for the other and both for God.'" That was your feeling at marriage. But when the new life comes, the language should be more inclusive. "Each for the other and the *three* for God." Your child will come *into* your solemn marriage covenant. You will place your little one in the very heart of your love for God and for each other. There he and all will grow strong, confident, happy.

Traits That Make for Marital Happiness or Unhappiness

Dr. Roy Burkhart in *From Friendship to Marriage,* had collected data on the causes of happy marriages and the causes of unhappy ones. This study he calls a "yardstick." In the study, one thousand families were questioned as to what qualities made their marriage a success, or if it were a failure, what they believed made it so.

Let us look at Dr. Burkhart's important list.

"Qualities of My Wife That Make for Marital Happiness." (Listed in the order of importance.)

1. She is always clean and neat.
2. She dresses especially for me each evening before my arrival home.
3. She cooks well, plans good meals.
4. She is economical. *good*
5. She knows when to talk.
6. She makes me want to please her.
7. She is a wonderful companion.
8. She is my complete mate.
9. She is free with her expressions of affection.
10. She is religious but not prudish.

These are revealing, and they are only a few of the statements. They show the many things that enter into family life in the everyday give and take. How about looking at the husband's side?

1. He does little thoughtful things that I do not have a right to expect.
2. He keeps well-groomed. *good*
3. He tells me interesting things about his work.
4. He is sympathetic about my physical disturbances. He understands.
5. He senses when I want affection and when I don't.
6. He always cleans the tub or basin after washing.
7. He kisses me before he leaves.
8. He notices little changes I make in the home.
9. He is identified with the church and other worthwhile organizations.
10. He never discusses my weak points in public.
11. He is tender and thoughtful in our love relations.
12. He can do handy things about the house.
13. He is not bored to stay home in the evening.
14. He never reminds me of his mother's cooking.

Here we have the woman's evaluation of those qualities she believes help to make a happy home. Can we not definitely say that these should be—but often are not—qualities of the Christian? We see the qualities that should characterize every born-again person: thoughtfulness, tenderness, co-operation, love, humility, consideration.

How would you like to see the admissions of failure listed by the five hundred unhappy men and women as they put down those things which in their estimation, have spoiled their married life?

1. She is always finding fault.
2. She opposes me in all I try to do. *Bad*
3. She is always clinging to her mother.
4. She is always fighting with the children.

5. She gets home often after I do and so I must wait for supper.
6. The home is always in an uproar.
7. She is always telling me I don't love her any more.
8. She uses extreme face paint and nail polish.
9. She gets on my nerves.

This is only a partial list, little things that grew big enough to spoil happiness. We add the other side for balance:

1. He leaves a ring in the tub.   *Bad*
2. He refuses to do anything about the house.
3. He is grouchy with the children.
4. He is stingy with his family, but liberal with others.
5. He is selfish.
6. He can't take criticism.
7. He insists on going to his mother's every Sunday evening.
8. He takes pride in scoffing at religion.
9. He shifts all the blame on me for our failures.
10. He is always alone with his thoughts.

Here we find the terrible power of the negative in life. Each is the opposite of Christian grace.

Taking these lists as a whole, they reveal character traits, selfishness or unselfishness, patience or impatience, fairness or unfairness, love or lack of love, and so on down through the list which, to those who penned them into the questionnaire were either testimonies of joy or admissions of despair. Each single sentence is a revelation of the human behavior pattern. May God help us to change our lives to conform to the profession we make.

Happiness in Marriage

Marriage is a rich and satisfying experience to those who are willing to sacrifice selfish ideas and patterns of action and work together to please Christ and each other. In the adjusting of two lives into a relationship of creative harmony, there are many trials, tears, heartaches and conflicts. Christian marriage is full of happiness but it is a happiness given by the Lord Jesus Christ to those who are willing to pay the price and deny themselves. Elsie Robinson, the journalist, has said something quite significant on this very point. We do not agree with her statement of marriage as a sacrament. Marriage is not a sacrament though it is holy, ordained of God and is a relationship upon which the blessing of almighty God rests in tenderest affection. We feel there is real, down-to-earth common sense in her remarks and such common sense as would revolutionize the thinking of many of our young people if it were carefully attended to. She says:

"It's my opinion that soft and pretty talk is what really fills the divorce courts. Little boys and girls read it and think they're going to make a go of marriage with candy hearts.

"There is probably no institution on earth about which more sacrilegious tripe is written. This notion, that matrimony consists of legalized romance, is the silliest and most dangerous fallacy ever foisted on the human race.

"I'm talking about real human beings who have the courage and audacity to live marriage as it is and was meant to be. The people who dare to be partners for life. Who dare to put aside their petty personal pattern, their pouts and peeves and quaking fears, and, kneeling, take the greatest Sacrament that God ever offered His children.

"What are your chances of a happy marriage? Practically nil. Unless you're willing to work at it as the greatest job of your life and not one you'll desert whenever you get your hair rumpled. Happiness and pleasure are pretty words. But they are the most poisonous things any human can experience as a steady diet. They'll make bums out of the bravest and finest people, either in or out of marriage. The Creator never meant people to be permanently happy here. People were invented for action and for service. And action and service always mean trouble.

"Am I belittling marriage? I am not. I am reverencing it. But I am trying to lift it out of the Valentine muck into which it has fallen and show it for what it is.

"Do I advise you to marry? I do, provided you're ready to face the works. If you want a kiddie game, buy yourself a flock of toy blocks. But if you can face marriage as men and women; if you can concentrate all you have of vision and courage, tenderness and loyalty and burning faith, then and only then have you the right to put your hand in God's and say, "I, too, will work with You."

"If you can't do that, you'd better not start monkeying around, or you'll be sorry. So think long, think hard, little Juliet and ardent Romeo, before you tackle something that was designed exclusively for those who will hold the line of marriage until the General says, "Rest now, thou good and faithful servant. Thou hast fought a good fight . . . thou hast finished the course . . . thou hast kept the faith . . . enter unto the peace of thy God everlasting."

Rules for Happy Marriage

An unknown author has set forth twelve rules for a happy marriage. These rules may be profitably studied by every couple.

Don't ever both get angry at the same time.

Never talk at one another, either alone or in company.

Never speak loudly to one another, unless the house is on fire.

Never find fault unless it is perfectly certain that a fault has been committed, and always speak lovingly.

Never taunt with a mistake.

Never make a remark at the expense of each other.

Never part for a day without loving words to think of during absence.

Never meet without loving welcome.

Never let the sun go down upon anger or grievance.

Never let any fault that you have committed go by, until you have frankly confessed it and asked forgiveness.

Never forget the happy hours of early love.

Never sigh over what might have been, but make the best of what is.

Personality Qualities

It is impossible to make a list of all the qualities that enter into our personalities as positive factors for a happy and successful marriage. It is worth while, however, to consider some of the outstanding personality qualities which have so much to do with happy, creative living together and qualities which the Holy Spirit longs to bring into full manifestation in every Christian life (Eph. 2:10). Each of these qualities may serve as a goal for personality development and also for the training of the children.

Colossians 3:8-10, 12-14; Galatians 5:16-25

Positive Qualities	Negative Qualities
1. Prayerful, looking to Christ, dependent on Him.	1. Prayerless, looking to self, dependent on self, independent of God
2. Cheerful, joyous, optimistic	2. Gloomy, morose, pessimistic, bitter
3. Friendly, agreeable, cooperative	3. Repellent, unsociable, disagreeable

4. Tolerant, generous, possessing a sense of humor	4. Opinionated, intolerant, unkind
5. Kind, courteous, tactful	5. Rude, untactful, harsh
6. Teachable, seeking to learn	6. Stubborn, set, unteachable
7. Loyal.	7. Unfaithful
8. Having convictions deeply rooted	8. Uncertain, having many ideas but none deeply rooted so as to grip the will, attitudes, and heart
9. Having high ideals, exalted goals	9. Having low standards, no goals that challenge
10. Self-denying	10. Egotistical, vain
11. Meek	11. Domineering
12. Reserved, careful, thoughtful	12. Aggressive, careless, thoughtless
13. Courageous, firm	13. Timid, fearful, weak
14. Honest, sincere, straightforward	14. Deceitful, evasive, misleading
15. Patient, calm, steady	15. Explosive, excitable
16. Happy, hopeful	16. Moody, depressed, hopeless
17. Moderate, balanced	17. Being an extremist, immoderate
18. Judicious, fair, discerning	18. Prejudiced, dominated by emotional likes and dislikes, driven by unexamined theories
19. Loving God above all and seeking to please Him in every action	19. Living for self and seeking to please self, not concerned with the glory of God

20. Sharing, seeking to share Christ's wonderful salvation with others	20. Selfishly embracing Christ, not concerned that others should know Him as Lord and Saviour
21. Growing into Christ's likeness and image	21. Having uncertain spiritual growth, up today, down tomorrow
22. Generous, open-hearted, forgiving	22. Resentful, unforgiving, grudgeholding
23. Neat, orderly, systematic	23. Disorderly, no system, no concern for neatness.
24. Having a smiling face	24. Having a frowning face
25. Pleasant, pleasing voice	25. Possessing a harsh, coarse voice
26. Possessing a spiritual experience characterized by peace, love, joy, faith	26. Having a spiritual experience characterized by conflict, morbidness, fear, selfishness, hate
27. Genuinely interested in God's Word	27. Having no concern for the Word of God, an attitude of indifference
28. Having a radiant, happy, forward look, full of hope and expectancy	28. Having a worried, morbid, backward look full of despair, disappointment

For Times of Sorrow

Times of sorrow, depression, and melancholy come to all men. "In the world ye shall have tribulation." There will be times when the problems of home life will seem to overwhelm. There may be misunderstandings, illness, death, financial reverses, temperamental and personality differences difficult to adjust and spiritual problems difficult to solve. What may be done to relieve the mind and ease the heart?

The story is told of an oriental king who had spells of deep depression and melancholia. One day, determined to be cured of these "spells," he called all the wise men of his kingdom together and demanded, "Tell me of a cure for sorrow and for depression of spirit." The wise men begged for time that they might consider the problem together. After a number of days' conference together they came back to the king and when asked for their answer said, "In times of sorrow and depression of spirit think, 'This too will pass.' "

This represents about the best counsel that can be given by the world. But the real answer is in Christ. He is the only answer that meets the need and truly satisfies. The answer of the Lord Jesus to this problem is not a saying or a philosophy or some moral platitude. Christ's answer is a Person, the Person of the Holy Spirit.

John 14:16, "And I will pray the Father, and he shall give you another Comforter, that he may abide with you forever."

Dr. R. A. Torrey, in a passage of rare beauty and penetrating insight, testifies to the comforting power of the Holy Spirit in a time of sorrow and depression of spirit. Dr. Torrey had just laid the body of his little girl away to await the great resurrection morning. She had been ill but seemed to be recovering, and so her death came unexpectedly, bringing a shocking grief to her parents.

Dr. Torrey says: "We carried the little body to the cemetery. It was raining pitilessly and as the little body was lowered into the grave and the rain poured upon the box that contained the casket, my wife turned to me and said:

'Archie, I am so glad that Elizabeth is not in that box!'"

"When we returned home, the health officers demanded, very wisely, that after being fumigated we should leave the house to them and go to a strange hotel for the night. All that night there was the most prolonged thunderstorm, except one, that I ever passed through. It seemed to be one unceasing flash of lightning and crash of thunder, and we could not sleep.

"The next morning as I went, thoroughly worn out, to the Bible Institute to meet my classes, as I passed around the corner of Chestnut Street and La Salle Avenue, I could contain my grief no longer. There was no one on the street, and I cried aloud, 'Oh, Elizabeth! Elizabeth!' And just then this fountain [the Holy Spirit] that I had in my heart broke forth with such power as I think I had never experienced before, and it was the most joyful moment that I had ever known in my life. Oh, how wonderful is the joy of the Holy Ghost! It is an unspeakably glorious thing to have your joy, not in things about you, not even in your most dearly loved friends, but to have within you a fountain ever springing up, springing up, springing up, always springing up, three hundred and sixty-five days in every year, springing up under all circumstances into everlasting life."

In times of sorrow, then, the blessed Holy Ghost will be your fountain of joy; He will break up the great deeps of sorrow and melancholy and will cause the waters of joy to flow and to overflow till in joy unspeakable and full of glory you wonder at the love, mercy, and grace of God! His promise will not fail; His promise is true! "In the last day, that great day of the feast, Jesus stood and cried, saying, If any man thirst, let him come unto me, and drink. He that believeth on me, as the scripture hath said, out of his belly [heart] shall flow rivers of living water. But this spake he of the Spirit which they that believe on him should

57

receive. . . . " (John 7:37-39). Let us then look to our Saviour, trusting Him implicitly to solve our problems and to the Holy Spirit to comfort and give of His joy. It is the sweet ministry of the Holy Spirit to glorify Christ (John 16:13, 14). As He glorifies Christ and makes Him real to our hearts, we shall know the peace of God midst times of deepest sorrow; and as He takes of the things of Christ and shows them to us, our hearts leap within us for the joy of a vigorous faith that makes us "more than conquerors."

Marriage Has Three Basic Stages

There seem to be three stages of development through which married life must go.

The first phase of married life is characterized by the fact that each one of the two partners recognizes in the other his ideal who harmonizes with his life needs. Everyone is familiar with this stage when in the first days of courtship and marriage each partner thinks the other is a walking personification of perfection. This attitude reveals the unity of heart.

In the second stage the husband and wife become aware of the need of a second kind of unity, unity of temperament, attitude, idea, and personality. This may be called for short, life-unity. This unity must be achieved as husband and wife work together in the common everyday tasks and problems of their married life. It is at this stage that young married couples begin to recognize the great difference between "heart-unity" and "life-unity." They begin to see the differences between themselves in attitude, temperament, practical ideas, and personality patterns. It is then that they begin to tell us that their marriage partner "seems" no longer the same. They are then tempted to bury their beautiful dreams about each other and they explain away their once beautiful unity of heart by saying it was only an idle, childish dream. It is tragedy when this happens, for then there is destroyed the one practical basis of inspiration for them, in their love for each other, while the difficult days of working out a unity of life to life are passing on. Let married couples in this stage frequently affirm before God the indivisible unity of their hearts to each other in love.

Then a third phase approaches in which the two partners begin to realize a deep unity of life. If they have yielded themselves to the Holy Spirit in their living together, they will find that He has, through the conflicts and differences of their temperaments, attitudes and personalities, brought about a transformation in both lives. Their respective attitudes and personalities will have been so transformed that the two lives will become one. Each will under His direction yield up its selfishness and dross, and each will receive of the good of the other. Through this process of give and take, each will grow into the beautiful harmony of two lives in one. This is not a bit of wishful thinking, but it is something that happens in most Christian marriages, as any faithful pastor can testify.

Those who refuse to yield themselves up to the transformations of this growth of two lives into one will of course find themselves growing farther and farther apart. If pastors will clearly point out the difference between heart-unity and life-unity and the process which leads to it, we believe much needless fear and sorrow would be spared young married couples. Many for lack of understanding never reach the third stage, or if they do reach it, do so after the loss of much precious time.

A Danger to Be Avoided

No person is free from faults. It should not surprise us to find faults in our loved one. The important thing is not whether or not we find the faults, but what we do with them when we discover them. It is possible for a husband to dwell so much on his wife's few faults that he becomes utterly blind to her many good qualities. It is possible to take two pennies and put one over each eye so as to shut out from view the beautiful landscape, the blooming flower, or the majestic mountain. For two cents one can lose sight of a million dollar's worth of value.

We know of a woman whose husband did not hang up his clothing as he should. This trait is aggravating to a wife who is neat and tidy, and she "nagged" him constantly in regard to it until she lost sight of the fact that her husband was a good provider; ambitious and getting ahead in his business; gentle and kindly in the home, deeply spiritual, and an earnest worker in the Lord's service.

We knew a man who nagged so much about his wife's cooking that he became blind to the fact that she was a wonderful mother, an efficient housekeeper, a sweet personality, and a true and devoted mate.

It will help if we will remember our own faults when we are prone to think too much about the faults of our loved one. And then let us be as kind and generous to our loved one as we are to ourselves.

Appreciation

The heart of a beautiful marriage is appreciation. The smile with which husband and wife meet each other at the end of a busy day, when things have gone wrong; the loving kiss which they place on each other's lips and the tender word of greeting can make the hardship of a disappointing day drop away. There are so many, many things that husband and wife may be genuinely thankful for in each other. One lovely Christian wife told her dearest friend that every day her husband thanks her and commends her for the things she does about the house. She said that even if she made mistakes, he would find something even about her mistakes for which to commend her. No wonder that home was a bit of heaven on earth.

One minister testifies that his father would go out early in the morning and find the most beautiful rosebud in the garden "and put it at mother's place to greet her when she came to breakfast." When he stepped behind her chair and gave her his morning kiss the whole day was glorified. Even if the children had gotten out of bed on the wrong side and had come downstairs in a mood to quarrel, they felt ashamed because the life of their home had been touched by the beauty of a thoughtful and gracious love! This little family lived close to the line of genuine poverty, yet the home was radiant because of the love of the father.

You remember the story of the wretched, weary tramp slumping on the park bench, confused and unhappy. A lovely child came and touched him, and said, "God loves you, and I love you, too!" That message brought the tramp to his feet, a saved and redeemed man. Why? Paul said, "We love him because he first loved us."

The great apostle John said, "Little children, let us love one another."

Appreciation is love at work. And appreciation will never fail to inspire, encourage and bless, for "love never faileth."

A Technique for Conflict

Conflict may be either good or bad. It may be the medium of a rich growth of meaning and value, provided the correct spiritual attitudes are maintained by husband and wife. If husband and wife maintain the proper spiritual attitude, the Holy Spirit will make conflict a creative experience. Creative conflict enlarges the mental horizons; enriches the resources of wisdom in the life; humbles and destroys arrogance, and opens the way for genuine growth of mind and soul. The idea that the issue is between harmful conflict and no conflict is wrong; conflict is sure to come, and if it is considered as bad, it will yield nothing but harm. If two strong personalities believe conflict is harmful, they may by vigorous efforts of the will repress all conflict and never take issue with each other. The results are always disastrous, for genuine differences are imbedded, and the two personalities grow farther and farther apart. Their world becomes an artificial world of make-believe, and their personalities become stunted and growth becomes an impossibility. The real issue is between bad conflict and good conflict.

Points for Good Conflict

1. Pray before you discuss. If you find yourself launched full tide in discussion of conflicting points of view before you have had time or thought for prayer, move to stop the discussion. Later when you have time, ask God to guide the conflict and to make it creative of real mental and spiritual values. Ask the Holy Spirit to glorify the Lord Jesus Christ in the thoughts that are exchanged. Nothing will do more toward insuring a proper spiritual tone in the conflict.

2. Express your ideas clearly and forcibly, but not in hostility or a nasty temper.

3. Introduce new ideas and helpful points of view that keep the discussion moving forward rather than in circles.

4. Encourage your loved one to present his or her ideas as clearly as possible, for the better able he is to present his case in it's best light, the more likely you will be to learn something that will enrich your mental and spiritual experience. Be eager to learn something new from your loved one's remarks.

5. After you have each presented your ideas as clearly as you know how, let the discussion terminate there. Do not seek to win the argument. Seek rather to grow by it. Leave

the result with Christ. Then affirm your love to each other and pray.

Some Don't's

1. Don't become discouraged over conflict. Your loved one still loves you. You will both be wiser and better for the exchange if you offer it up to the Lord Jesus Christ with a prayer that He bless it to your good and your growth.

2. Don't sulk or pout.

3. Don't become moody, bad-tempered, irritable, or have an anger tantrum. This reveals a selfish spirit and a closed mind.

4. Don't evade conflict unless you feel the proper conditions are not present to make it profitable. Face conflict squarely, frankly, fearlessly. Then conflict becomes a valuable means of growth in marriage.

5. If you become angry, keep quiet.

6. Don't scold, nag, or carry grudges in a sullen manner, nor compete with your loved one in irritability.

A LITTLE LONGER

Oh, to be in Jesus's bosom,
 There to hide my pain and care,
There to feel His arms around me,
 All my trouble ended there!

Oh, to be in quiet lying
 On His peace-insuring breast,
There forgetting sin and sorrow,
 There forevermore at rest!

Ties that hold us here, unknotted
 In the faith we there must know —
Willing, in His trusted presence,
 To let earthly dear things go:

Willing to resign the dearest,
  Even the flesh of our flesh born,
Even the baby, in our dying
  Left so humanly forlorn!

Ah! I feel his tiny fingers
  Reaching helplessly to me;
Let me still a little longer
  Painful, sorrowing, troubled be;

So I yet may be his comfort,
  Shield him from the bitter cold,
Lead him by my guiding counsel
  To a tender Saviour's fold!

Not until my task is ended,
  Task of toil or agony,
Would I close my weary eyelids
  And in bliss forever be:

Not until life's work is finished
  Would I seek the perfect rest
That awaits the poor believer,
  Sinking tired on Jesus' breast.

                              —Mary B. Dodge

5

THE CHRISTIAN MOTHER

The Greatest Wonder of God's Creation

MOTHER! Sweet, tender, glorious name! A name that never fails to remind us of the faithful and ever enduring mercies of Christ. She is midst all God's creation—His masterpiece! Bishop Thompson has described a mother in beautiful words: "Mother! How many delightful associations cluster around that word! The innocent smiles of infancy, the gambols of boyhood, and the happiest hours of riper years! When my heart aches at the world's wickedness, and my limbs are weary and my feet bloody, traveling the thorny path of life, I am accustomed to sit down on some mossy stone, and closing my eyes on real scenes, send my spirit back to the days of early life. I sing my lullaby, or watch my goldfinch, or catch my rabbits, or watch the streets of my native city, or look over the green; I hear the shrill bugle and view the prancing cavalry, or go down to the dockyard, or walk along the seashore, or prattle with my brother, and kiss my sweet sister; I feel afresh my infant joys and sorrows, till my spirit recovers its tone, and is willing to pursue its journey. But in all these reminiscences my mother rises. If I seat myself upon my cushion, it is at her side; if I sing, it is to her ear; if I walk the walls or the meadows, my little hand is in my mother's, and my little feet keep company with hers; if I stand and listen to the piano, it is because my mother's fingers touch the keys; if I survey the wonders of creation, it is my mother who points out the object of my admiring attention; if a hundred cannon pronounce a national salute, I find myself clinging to her knees. When my heart bounds with its best joys, it is because at the performance of some task, or the recitation of some verses, I receive a present from her hand. There is no velvet so soft as a mother's lap, no rose so lovely as her smile, no path so flowery as that imprinted with her footsteps."

The Influence of Mother

Mothers have tremendous influence. Who can measure the length and breadth of Mother's influence—whether for God or Satan; heaven or hell; joy or sorrow; strength or weakness! Before the child is born he lives by mother's heart and after he is born he lives by her guiding hand. One old divine, showing the influence of mothers and how they live on in their children, said, "Mothers live in the lives of their children. When John came forth on his great mission, behold how the leading characteristics of his mother developed themselves in him. He stands on the banks of the Jordan, in whose tide he had baptized hundreds of candidates on a profession of their repentance for sin and faith in the coming of the Messiah. A new Candidate approaches and asks baptism. John recognizes in the new Candidate his Lord and Master, and with deep humility says, 'I have need to be baptized of thee, and wherefore comest thou to me?' Of what do these words remind you? Remember what Elisabeth said to Mary before the birth of either of their sons, when she used almost this identical language in her humble exclamation, 'Whence is this to me, that the mother of my Lord, should come to me?' See you not the mother's humility living in her son?

"Another trait in Elisabeth's character was the devotedness of her piety. It burned with a quenchless altar flame. She did not, like Sarah, doubt the promise of God, and was it not said of her son that 'he was a bright and a shining light'?

"She also developed great fortitude and moral courage. And did not her son develop all the high elements of moral heroism? Remember his withering denunciations of sin and willful sinners! Remember his scathing rebuke of Herod's wicked life.

"O! mothers, learn your duty and privilege!"

"O say to mothers what a holy charge
 Is theirs! With what a queenly power their love
Can rule the fountain of the new-born mind!
 Warn them to wake at early dawn and sow
Good seed before the world hath sown her tares:
 Not in their toil decline, that angel bands
May put their sickles in and reap for God
 And gather in His garner."

 ## MY MOTHER

My mother is my heart's ideal
 Of all that's dear and good.
Her life is radiant with love
 And gracious womanhood.
She's sympathetic, gentle, kind;
 She understands a lad;
And oh, she's just the truest friend
 A fellow ever had!

My mother never turns me down
 Or fails me when in need.
To sacrifice herself and serve
 Her loved ones is her creed.

She practices her faith in God
  With joy and eagerness:
Her ministry's a miracle
  Of sweet unselfishness.

My mother is my friend of friends;
  She's all the world to me!
I owe her everything I am
  And all I hope to be.
I want to live a life like hers,
  And oh, I want to prove
Myself deserving of her faith
  And worthy of her love!

—Selected

The mother's place being of such influence, she is responsible to see that her influence is always at its best for God. Dr. R. A. Torrey says in a powerful sermon on the importance of motherhood: "There is no nobler occupation upon earth, no higher calling than that of being a mother, a true mother. This Book which I hold in my hand confers great honor upon motherhood. The ideal woman of the Bible is not a woman who goes around making speeches, is not a woman who belongs to clubs, is not a woman that occupies a public position. The ideal woman of the Bible is the mother. That is the highest position a woman can occupy. . . . The most blessed of all women, the Virgin Mary, was a mother. Nobody can tell the amount of good that can be accomplished by a true mother. Nobody can tell the amount of evil that can be accomplished by a bad mother."

Nothing is more beautiful than a pattern mother; but on the other hand, nothing is more pathetic than a prodigal mother. I always remember a faithful member of the first church at which I was pastor, telling me that his father and mother were drunken wastrels. Even as a boy he used to pray, "O Lord, save me from being like my parents."

Susannah Wesley a Practical Inspiration

Susannah Wesley was an ideal mother, who knew how to translate her idealism into daily practical values. Every mother should desire to be the best kind of mother, and it is the desire of every Christian mother to find ways and means to best discharge her responsibilities. We give here Susannah Wesley's twenty-one principles and rules by which she reared her family. We believe every mother will gain practical help and encouragement from a careful study of her principles. These were set forth (all but the last one) in a letter to her son John on July 24, 1732. In a previous letter to him she had warned, "No one can without renouncing the world in the most literal sense, observe my method; and there are few, if any, that would entirely devote above twenty years of the prime of life in hopes to save the souls of their children, which they think may be saved without so much ado; for that was my principal intention, however unskillfully and unsuccessfully managed."

Her rules and principles are as follows (most of these are just as she wrote them to her son):

1. The children were always put into a regular method of living, in such things as they were capable of, from their birth; as in dressing and undressing, changing their linen, and so on. The first quarter commonly passes in sleep. After that they were, if possible, laid into their cradle awake, and rocked to sleep; and so they were kept rocking till it was time for them to awake. This was done to bring them to a regular course of sleeping, which at first was three hours in the morning and three in the afternoon; afterward two hours, till they needed none at all.

2. When turned a year old (and some before), they were

taught to fear the rod and to cry softly; by which means they escaped abundance of correction which they might otherwise have had; and that most odious noise of the crying of children was rarely heard in the house, but the family usually lived in as much quietness as if there had not been a child among them.

3. As soon as they were grown pretty strong, they were confined to three meals a day. Whatever food they had, they were never permitted, at those meals, to eat of more than one thing, and of that sparingly enough. Drinking or eating between meals was never allowed, unless in case of sickness. They were never permitted to choose their meat but always made to eat such things as were provided for the family.

4. In order to form the minds of children, the first thing to be done is to conquer their will and bring them to an obedient temper. To inform the understanding is a work of time and must with children proceed by slow degrees as they are able to bear it; but the subjecting the will is a thing that must be done at once, and the sooner the better. For by neglecting timely correction they will contract a stubbornness and obstinacy which are hardly ever after conquered; and never, without using such severity as would be as painful to me as to the child. In the esteem of the world they pass for kind and indulgent, whom I call cruel, parents who permit their children to get habits which they know must be afterwards broken. . . .

Whenever a child is corrected, it must be conquered; and this will be no hard matter to do, if it be not grown headstrong by too much indulgence. And when the will of a child is totally subdued and it is brought to revere and stand in awe of the parents, then a great many childish follies and inadvertences may be passed by. Some should be overlooked and taken no notice of, and others mildly reproved; but no willful transgression ought ever to be forgiven children without chastisement, less or more, as the nature and circumstances of the case may require.

"I insist on the conquering of the will of children betimes, because this is the only strong and rational foundation of a religious education; without which both precept and example will be ineffectual. But when this is thoroughly done, then a child is capable of being governed by the reason and piety of its parents, till its own understanding comes to maturity and the principles of religion have taken root in the mind.

"I cannot yet dismiss the subject. As self-will is the root of all sin and misery, so whatever cherishes this in children insures their own after wretchedness and irreligion; whatever checks and mortifies it promotes their future happiness and piety. This is still more evident if we consider that religion is nothing else than doing the will of God and not our own. . . .

5. Our children were taught, as soon as they could speak, the Lord's Prayer, which they were made to say at rising and at bedtime constantly; to which, as they grew bigger, were added a short prayer for their parents and some collects; a short catechism and some portion of Scripture, as their memories could bear.

6. They were very early made to distinguish the Sabbath from other days, before they could well speak or go.

7. They were early taught to be still at family prayers and to ask a blessing immediately after, which they used to do by signs, before they could kneel or speak.

8. They were quickly made to understand they might have nothing they cried for and instructed to speak courteously for what they wanted. They were not permitted to ask even the lowest servant for aught without saying, 'Pray give me such a thing.'

9. Taking God's name in vain, cursing, swearing, pro-

fanity, obscenity, rude, ill-bred names were never heard among them. Nor were they ever permitted to call each other by their proper names without the addition of brother or sister.

10. There was no such thing as loud playing or talking allowed.

11. Every child was kept close to his business for the six hours of school each day. It is almost incredible what may be taught a child in a quarter of a year by a vigorous application if it have but a tolerable capacity and good health. . . .

12. After our house was rebuilt [because of fire] we began the system of the children singing Psalms at morning and evening. At five in the evening a general retirement was entered upon, when the eldest took the youngest that could speak, and the second the next, to whom they read the Psalms for the day and a chapter in the New Testament; as in the morning they were directed to read the Psalms and a chapter in the Old Testament, after which they went to their private prayers, before they got their breakfast or came into the family.

13. It had been observed that cowardice and fear of punishment often lead children into lying till they get a custom of it which they cannot leave. To prevent this, a law was made that whoever was charged with a fault of which they were guilty, if they would ingenuously confess it and promise to amend, should not be beaten. This rule prevented a great deal of lying. . . .

14. No sinful action, as lying, pilfering , . . . disobedience, quarreling, was ever permitted to pass unpunished.

15. No child was ever to be reprimanded or beaten twice for the same fault; and that if they amended, they should never be upbraided with it afterwards.

16. Every signal act of obedience, especially when it

crossed upon their own inclinations, should be always commended, and frequently rewarded according to the merits of the case.

17. If any child ever performed an act of obedience or did anything with an intention to please, though the performance was not well, yet the obedience and intention should be kindly accepted; and the child with sweetness directed how to do better for the future.

18. The rights of property must be invariably preserved and none suffered to invade the property of another in the smallest matter, though it were of the value of a farthing or a pin, which they might not take from the owner without, much less against, his consent. This rule can never be too much inculcated on the minds of children; and from the want of parents and governors doing it as they ought proceeds that shameful neglect of justice which we may observe in the world.

19. Promises must be strictly observed; and a gift once bestowed, and so the right passed away from the donor, be not resumed, but left to the disposal of him to whom it was given; unless it were conditional, and the condition of the obligation not performed.

20. No girl must be taught to work till she can read very well; and that she be kept to her work with the same application, and for the same time, that she was held to in reading.

Susannah Wesley gave each child an evening in the week during which time she counseled and encouraged him in the Word of God. John Wesley's evening was Thursday. He later testified how tremendous an influence this evening spent with his mother had on the forming of his mind and judgments. After he was away from her side he asked her to still devote this evening to his interest by praying for him.

John Wesley in his sermons on the religious education of children followed in the footsteps of his devout mother's teachings. Wesley taught there are four diseases to which children, as heirs of fallen Adam, are especially subject: self-will, love of world, pride, and atheism. In connection with each disease he set forth the Scriptural antidote.

1. Self-will. The child's will must be broken and subjected before he reaches the age of two years. He must know by then that his will must yield to the parents' word and authority. To give a child what it cries for is to humor it and is but to reward its will for self-assertion. Mrs. Wesley did not teach that the *will* must be broken but that self-will must be broken. Her teaching was actually to the end that the will of the child may be freed from the imprisoning slavery of self and selfishness, that it may be free to conform to the commandments of God; these are for the best interests of the child and of those who must live and work with him now and later. Self-will makes the child a law unto himself, thus leading to godlessness, delinquency, criminality, frustrations of all kinds, and general inability to get along with other people. Thus we see why God says that the parent who refuses to chastise his child hates him.

2. Love of the world

Parents are not to adorn their children with such frills and gew-gaws as other children wear simply that they may look prettier. Parents are not to encourage their children to outdo others in dress or in other ways, and thus build up the strength of envy, jealousy, and hatred in them. It is this that is the very heart of "worldliness."

3. Pride

Wesley warned against the praise of children for other than religious and spiritual worth. To praise them apart from God is to feed their natural sense of pride. To strike at the root of pride, children are to be taught *early* that they are fallen spirits, fallen short of that glorious image of God. They are now like Satan in possessing pride, passion, revenge, envy, and jealousy. This self-knowledge, under the Holy Spirit, leads to real conviction for sin and a sense of need for Christ and His salvation. The child will be brought to realize that all his gifts and talents he owes to the grace, mercy, and love of Christ.

4. Atheism

Atheism is the result of neglect on the part of parents in daily teaching and training the child. A *spirit* of atheism—observing, treating with, and only thinking about *second causes* is fostered in the child because he is not deeply taught, both by example and precept, the truth of God, who is the *First Cause*.

UNSPOKEN PRAYER

Too tired, too worn to pray,
   I can but fold my hands;
Entreating in a voiceless way,
   Of Him who understands
How flesh and heart succumb—
   How will sinks, weary, weak.

Dear Lord, my languid lips are dumb;
   See what I cannot speak.
Just as the wearied child,
   Through sobbing pain opprest,
Drops, hushing all its wailings wild,
   Upon its mother's breast;

So on Thy bosom, I
   Would cast my speechless prayer.
Nor doubt that Thou wilt let me lie

In trustful weakness there;
And though no conscious thought
  Before me rises clear,

The prayer of wordless language wrought,
  Thou yet wilt deign to hear;
For when, at best I plead—
  What so my spirit saith—
I only am the bruised reed,
  And Thou the breathing breath.

           —Margaret J. Preston

A MIDNIGHT HYMN

The authorship of the following beautiful hymn of trust is unknown. It was found treasured up in a humble cottage in England.

In the mild silence of the voiceless night,
When, chased by airy dreams the slumbers flee,
Whom in the darkness doth my spirit seek,
    O God, but Thee?

And if there be a weight upon my breast,
Some vague impression of the day foregone,
Scarce knowing what it is, I fly to Thee
    And lay it down.

So if it be the heaviness that comes
In token of anticipated ill,
My bosom takes no heed of what it is,
    Since 'tis Thy will.

For oh, in spite of past and present care,
Or anything besides, how joyfully
Passes that almost solitary hour,
    My God, with Thee!

More tranquil than the stillness of the night,
More peaceful than the silence of that hour,
More blest than anything my bosom lies
     Beneath Thy power.

For what is there on earth that I desire
Of all that it can give or take from me?
Or whom in heaven doth my spirit seek,
     O God! but Thee?

6

THE CHRISTIAN FATHER

Ephesians 6:4

FATHER! What a great word and with what a great meaning! To every serious man who is a father there comes the question, "How can I be the best father?"

Dr. Payson gives fathers an exhortation that seems to carry the challenge of Christ to every man occupying this high and exalted position.

"What if God should place in your hand a diamond, and tell you to inscribe on it a sentence which should be read at the last day, and shown there as an index of your own thoughts and feelings? What care, what caution would you exercise in the selection! Now, this is what God has done. He has placed before you the immortal minds of your children, more imperishable than the diamond; on which you are about to inscribe every day and every hour, by your instructions, by your spirit, or by your example, something which will remain, and be exhibited for or against you at the judgment day."

Some time ago Dr. John Holland, radio pastor, in an address at a father and son banquet, presented three words as forming the pattern of his message. His three words of counsel to fathers about their sons were, "*play* with him, *stay* with him and *pray* with him."

I. The Father Should Play with His Children

Mr. Average Father has for the most part lost contact

with the play-life of his children. F. A. Crosby says that it is the duty and privilege of a father to read with his boy, play with him, make things with him, talk baseball and football with him; to roam the woods and fields with him, as opportunity offers; to hunt, fish and swim with him; sharing such joys as these with his boy means the sharing of parent life and establishing a bond of attachment that will never break. Just the thought of these things will turn any home into a boys' "club."

The importance of play is not well enough realized by parents. Parents oftentimes look upon play as foolishness or as a waste of time. Nothing could be farther from the truth. Play is vital to the child and is closely related to his total physical, spiritual, and mental development. Children are mostly all muscle and this fact explains their desire for play. Nearly their whole life is built around their muscles; thus there must be action in their program. Nothing—neither love, room, good intentions, time, interest or adaptability—can take the place of action in a child's life. Action is the growing edge of their lives. Thus the vital importance for the father to make such a connection with the play or action life of his children as will make him a definite part of it.

Dr. G. E. Johnson in his book, *Education through Play and Games,* points out that it takes a human being almost one-third of his life to get ready to live, and that that one-third is spent mostly in play. Play thus becomes an important means of self- and life-discovery. Dr. Josiah Strong says: "The impulse to play is as natural and normal as the inclination to sleep or the desire to eat; and when we understand its true meaning, we find that it is not simply a permissible thing, but a divinely ordered thing. If God gives the impulse, fathers ought to provide the opportunity for expression of the impulse under the best sort of conditions.

If we wish our boys to develop habits of honesty, courtesy and unselfishnes, appreciation of justice and chivalry, we must provide opportunity for practice of these desirable characteristics."

What wonderful opportunity the father has to play with his children in swimming, hiking, coasting, skating, tennis, baseball, football, running, calisthenics, and indoor games of many kinds! As the children engage in vigorous play with their father, their personalities unfold and they grow in his likeness and image. The spiritual father will always seek throughout all the play to encourage and develop gallantry, honor, cleanness, kindness, respect, courtesy, ability to be a good loser, loyalty, bravery, and humility.

In such play activity, fathers and children really get acquainted with each other and the children come to have that deep sense of love and confidence in their father. Many a disobedient, uninterested, lazy child could be made alive with a new spirit overnight if father would try "playing with him" for only a month. Fathers, try it and see the difference in them and in you!

II. The Father Should Spend Time with His Children

Roger W. Babson tells of a prominent man who became greatly concerned about his boy, and consequently went to the boy's school principal and asked for suggestions. The principal gave this very significant reply: "Resign from the presidency of the Chamber of Commerce. Leave that position to someone whose family has grown up and is not in such great need of fatherly attention as is your boy. Your first duty during the next five years, after providing the necessities of life for your family, is at home with your boy. You should help him with his lessons; you should interest him in your business; and you should become his comrade and chum. By giving the same amount of time and attention to your boy that you now give to the Chamber of Commerce, you will save your boy and also probably be the means of doing just as much good for your city. The future of every city and the future of your boy depend primarily upon giving him your personal attention. In fact, is not personal attention necessary to make any work successful?"

E. Mitchell Hodges tells the story of his meeting a very prosperous businessman. In the course of the conversation the businessman said, "Would you like to know what I'm giving my boy for Christmas?" Hodges said, "Yes." The businessman pulled out his wallet and took from it a piece of paper with the following written on it.

"To my dear Son! I give to you one hour of each weekday and two hours of my Sunday to be yours, to be used as you want it without interference of any kind whatsoever."

Hodges thought, "I wonder what that boy will feel and think when on Christmas morning he looks at that slip of paper. If he is the average boy, he will be very much dissatisfied. If he is an unusual boy, he will realize that his father has given him something that he can never repay."

"How did you happen to reach the decision to give that present?" Hodges asked. He said, "One day I was seated in my office and a human derelict came in to see me, and when he mentioned his name I said, 'Lad, to see you like this—and you with such a father!' 'Well, I have often heard said that he was a fine man,' the boy answered. 'All his friends have said so. I never knew him. He was so occupied with his business and with his associations that I only saw him occasionally at meals. I never knew him.'

" 'That made me think, and so I am going to concentrate my time on having my boy know me.' " It costs to be a real father to one's child; it costs *time*, love, patience, money and *time*. We emphasize time, for there is where the real lack is. The time is not taken.

Edgar Guest in his story, *What My Father Did for Me,* shows clearly what wonderful possibilities stand before the father as he stays with his child in those hours of loving communion of heart with heart. He says: "During our walks together, he had a way of calling my attention to men he wanted me to know, and always he talked about them. He seemed to be acting as a pair of magnifying glasses for me, enlarging the good qualities of others that I might see them clearly. I never saw a great man without my father's explaining to me why he was great, nor a bad man without being made to understand what made him bad. In that way I learned what traits to acquire and what faults to avoid. He was teaching me by example, and I didn't know I was being taught." He goes on to reveal the treasures a dad may discover to his child as he "stays with him." "I have made good friends and true, because my father taught me how lasting friendships are made. . . . I have found much happiness in life, because he taught me where happiness could be found.

"I have traveled not far, but safely, because he taught me wisely.

"I have been spared regret and shame and misery and the embarrassment of countless follies by the tact and genius of his counsel; and scarcely a day goes by, even now, that I do not discover in my heritage from him, some new vein of riches."

Oh! the opportunity a father has to lay before the child's developing mind the excellencies there are in our Lord and Saviour Jesus Christ! In these times he stays with his children. Those fathers who fail to avail themselves of these priceless opportunities will never hear "Well done!" either from their children or from their Saviour!

III. The Father Should Pray with His Children

In Ephesians 6:4, God gives a specific commandment to fathers. How many fathers obey this commandment? I have often contended that no child should ever be spanked if the father is not obedient to the command in Ephesians 6:4. Much of childhood disobedience can be traced to the parents' disobedience of the command in Ephesians 6:4 and the promise in Proverbs 22:6. In this Ephesian passage the Holy Spirit plainly implies that fathers who do not train their children in the nurture and admonition of the Lord are guilty of "provoking them to anger" (which is the root of disobedience very frequently). Weymouth beautifully renders this verse: "Fathers, do not irritate your children, but bring them up tenderly with true Christian training and advice."

On this verse, Calvin says:

"Parents on the other hand are exhorted not to irritate their children by unreasonable severity. [Author's note: That is, severity which is punishment of children *without* a faithful, loving training of them, as in daily family worship and personal companionship and counsel. Some fathers are handy with the rod of the wood but very unskillful with the rod of the Word. This is a rebuke to them from the Holy Spirit.] This would excite hatred, and would lead them to throw off the yoke altogether. Accordingly, in writing to the Colossians, he adds, 'lest they be discouraged' (Col. 3:21). Kind and liberal treatment has rather a tendency to cherish reverence for their parents, and to increase the cheerfulness and activity of their obedience, while a harsh and unkind manner rouses them to obstinacy, and destroys the natural affections; but Paul goes on to say, 'Let them be fondly cherished'; for the Greek word . . . which is translated *bring up*, unquestionably conveys the idea of gentleness and forbearance. To guard them, however, against the opposite and frequent evil of excessive indulgence, he again draws the reign which he had slackened, and adds 'in the instruction and reproof of the Lord.' It is not the will of God that parents in the exercise of kindness, shall spare and corrupt their children. Let their conduct towards their children be at once mild and considerate, so as to guide them in the fear of the Lord, and correct them also when they go astray."

A father's duty is to lead his children to Christ. All his spiritual efforts must be directed to this end.

In this it is best for mothers to concentrate on the daughters and the fathers on the sons, but with both parents always giving a clear testimony to the need and necessity of salvation through Christ. The father will find opportune moments—openings made by the Holy Spirit—for him to press the invitation upon the child. At how early an age can this be done?

If the child is reared around a family altar, and if the child has a sense of fellowship and confidence in the father, he may then be led to Christ very early. We would say as early as two, and surely this tremendous decision should not be put off by the child after he is five. A faithful mother or father who follows the principles taught in this book can lead his children to Christ before they are five!

After the child has accepted Christ, the father will pray *with* him. It will be the delight of the child's heart to have father pray with him about his problems. The father in these times of spiritual ministry to his children will find himself sharing many of the children's inmost fears, doubts, and problems. The teacher at school; the lessons so hard to understand; the children—some friendly and some mean and naughty—any or all these experiences and problems in their life they are most likely to share with father in these intimate, holy times of spiritual fellowship.

The sight of father praying and reverently talking of the things of God, and hearing father as he sets forth needed counsels and encouragements, will never be forgotten.

Gypsy Smith speaks most beautifully of his father's life and example. He says: "Our first idea of God came from Father's beautiful life in the Gypsy tent—a life which was like the blooming of a flower, whose beauty won us all. If Father had lived one life in a meeting and another in the Gypsy tent, he would not have been able to rejoice today over his five children converted. But the beauty of Father's character was most seen in his home life. We dearly loved to have him all to ourselves. Nobody knew as well as we children what a fine, magnificent character he was. Whenever we were tempted to do things that were at all doubtful, we at once thought of Father, and if we had any suspicion that the course of conduct we contemplated would not be pleasing to him, we at once abandoned all idea of following it."

Someone has said that three per cent of a child's sense impressions come through his sense of touch, taste and smell. Twelve per cent of his sense impressions come through his sense of hearing, and eighty-five per cent through his sense of sight! Thus the power of such a holy example!

The blessings of a spiritual father can never fully be measured or known this side the great judgment seat of Christ. We think of Zacharias, the spiritually minded father of John the Baptist. When John was born his father folded him to his bosom and, looking with inexpressible tenderness upon the babe, he spoke those wondrous words of divine illumination (Luke 1:68-79) that close with a father's loving benediction and heartfelt dedication of his son (Luke 1:76-79). "And thou, child, shalt be called the

85

prophet of the Highest: for thou shalt go before the face of the Lord to prepare his ways;

"To give knowledge of salvation unto his people by the remission of their sins, through the tender mercy of our God; whereby the dayspring from on high hath visited us, to give light to them that sit in darkness and in the shadow of death, to guide our feet into the way of peace."

What a benediction and dedication of son by father! When—after he had reached the age of three or four? *Ah, no! at John's birth!* Is this not a worthy example for every spiritual father to follow? What Zacharias did then set the tone and atmosphere of all his ministry of God to his son in the years following. Quite naturally it followed that "the child grew, and waxed strong in spirit" (Luke 1:80). For lack of parental love and true spiritual guidance, the children are paying a terrible price.

If fathers (and mothers) will not devote special time each day to their children, they may rest assured the world, the flesh and the devil will. We quote words from an editorial in *The Herald of His Coming* that should stir every parent to action.

"Have you ever seen a drunk fifteen-year-old boy? You may not, if you lead secluded lives away from the pulse of American youth. But again you may, for there are from two to three times as many of them in 1951 as there were in 1941. You can hardly believe other facts about the average American fifteen-year-old boy: that he, at his tender years, is supposed to have enough knowledge of contraceptives and prophylactics to keep him from 'getting into trouble'; that federal agents investigating wide-spread marijuana and heroin addiction among schoolchildren find too many of them under sixteen years of age.

"'Alcoholics Unanimous!' is the warning of Dr. John Almack, Stanford University professor. 'So we're going if the present trend continues! About fifty per cent of high school and college students use alcohol, and it is becoming a problem among junior high students thirteen and fourteen years old.'

"Do dry statistics about the soaring number of illegitimate births among our American girls go in one ear and out the other? Perhaps the jolt many of us need is to go to that hospital corridor and hear the piercing wail of a little thirteen-year-old girl in labor—frightened, panicky, bringing forth an unwanted baby in shame. Oh, the horror and pathos of those little American child-mothers, stumbling into maternity homes, hiding out for long months, facing alone an ordeal that is difficult enough surrounded by love and society's approval!

"What a grim day of reckoning is coming for all those hellish forces which conspired to put her there—from the liquor dealers to the Hollywood harlots, setting her an example of adultery; from the licentious comics publishers to the dance-crazy parents who placed her in temptation. Here is where 'finished sin' demands its cruel payment, where a sex-mad culture traps its little bewildered victims . . . So widespread is this problem in our land that public school systems in at least two states, Michigan and Minnesota, have assigned teachers to conduct regular classes among the young schoolgirls living in maternity homes.

"There are records of over 100,000 such misfortunes, but officials say, 'Make it three times that many, and you'll come closer to the truth.' Worse still is the growing number of grade-school girls each month, each year, entering these homes! Weep, weep, America! Isn't this worse than the 'fixing' of basketball games which stunned and crushed officials and parents from coast to coast, and which brought such prompt disciplinary action!

"Gone forever is our right to be complacent as American

Christians. Only an alarmist can be a realist today! And while authorities frantically search for psychological causes and palliative measures—everything from a 'lack of security' to 'need for more recreation centers' and more 'courses in sex and marriage,' we know deep in our souls that this is a symptom of a moral and spiritual malady, far progressed. The only step forward for America is the step back to God!

"'A million youth for Christ this year!' is the bold, confident slogan of one of God's answers, Youth for Christ. There are so many practical courses of action which desperate and determined Christians must take to save their youth—prayer, the family altar and vigilant parental love and instruction is the number one need they require of us. Christian schools are springing up from coast to coast, requiring our financial assistance, whether we have children or not. Youth evangelism, planned programs of work and play, challenges to service—all are needed. May God help us to salvage this crucial generation!"

The Father's Responsibility Should Not Be Avoided

All too many fathers are seeking to avoid their responsibilities to their children, pleading that they are tired from the day's work or otherwise not capable.

Frederick Arnold Kummer writing in *Good Housekeeping* on "The Father in Child Training," makes splendid suggestions in regard to the responsibility of parents.

"The responsibility of the father in the training of the child is one he should welcome. It is not only unfair, but often inadequate, to leave the entire duty of home training to the mother. The growing child sees his father as a vastly important character, who vanishes from his little world early in the morning and usually returns to it in the evening, tired, hungry, with no time for his children except to bid them goodnight. This of course, is not right. Neither the child nor the father is getting out of their relationship what he should. If, but slowly, surely, the child grows up to exclude his father from his little world, what hope can there be of mutual understanding when the days of childhood are past and real problems take place of imaginary ones? The writer fully understands how little time the busy father usually has; but even a half-hour of intimate association with a child daily, a kindly interest in his affairs, a helping hand with his lessons, a suggestion as to the books he should read, would be of the utmost value in establishing a basis of comradeship."

Edgar A. Guest has given us some beautiful thoughts on what he considers to be his real job as a father. He says, "If I don't help my boy, Bud, to grow up right, I'll call myself a failure, no matter how much money I make, or how big a reputation I get.

"I have a number of tasks to do, all of which I should like to do well. To be a failure in any one of them would be disappointing; yet I could bear that without whimpering if I were sure I had not failed the boy . . . Not so much of me in the bank, and more of me and of my best in the lad, is what I should like to have to show at the end of my career . . . For me to succeed as a father, he must succeed. Unless my boy comes to manhood fit for the respect of his fellow men, I shall have been a failure. The glory of our handwork lies not in ourselves, but in our children." Edgar Guest relates his thoughts to the son but the same conclusions hold true whether the child be son or daughter.

THE BUILDER

A builder builded a temple;
  He wrought it with grace and skill;
Pillars and groins and arches
  All fashioned to work his will.
Men said as they saw its beauty,
  "It shall never know decay;
Great is thy skill, O builder!
  Thy fame shall endure for aye."

A teacher builded a temple
  With loving and infinite care,
Planning each arch with patience,
  Laying each stone with prayer.
None praised his unceasing efforts,
  None knew of his wondrous plan,
For the temple the teacher builded
  Was unseen by the eyes of man.

Gone is the builder's temple,
  Crumbled into the dust;
Low lies each stately pillar,
  Food for consuming rust.
But the temple the teacher builded
  Will last while the ages roll,
For that beautiful unseen temple
  Was a child's immortal soul.

Author Unknown

7

FUNDAMENTAL CONTENT OF CHILD GUIDANCE

But continue thou in the things which thou hast learned and hast been assured of, knowing of whom thou hast learned them;

And that from a child thou hast known the holy scriptures, which are able to make thee wise unto salvation through faith which is in Christ Jesus.

All scripture is given by inspiration of God, and is profitable for doctrine, for reproof, for correction, for instruction in righteousness:

That the man of God may be perfect, thoroughly furnished unto all good works.

—II Timothy 3:14-17

Fundamental Content of Child Training Salvation

REV. ROY A. BREHM says: "Obviously the child's Christian experience begins with the acceptance of the Lord Jesus Christ as personal Saviour. Although he may be a good child, say his prayers, read his Bible, attend Sunday school and church and always obey his parents, he still needs the Saviour. As he recognizes himself to be a sinner and therefore in need of a Saviour, he then receives Christ into his heart. Thus he has a new life, Christ's own life and righteousness, to take the place of his own self-righteousness. This is the root and foundation of all further experience and growth in grace for all time and eternity."

We may say at this point that the receiving of Christ in the heart is the cornerstone of every happy, harmonious and spiritual marriage. It is noteworthy that of all the divorces that are granted every year around the world there will be extremely few if any divorces granted to couples where both profess to having received Christ into their hearts. We have never heard of one Christian family being broken up by divorce. When we see this truth, we realize how important and vital a step it is when one opens up his heart and invites the Lord Jesus to come in and abide forever. Christ comes in and brings new life, His own life, and in that new life of Christ there is all the grace, power, and understanding needed to make one a success, whether in marriage, business, or any other area of life.

Parents sometimes wonder if the little children under five are not too young to open their hearts and receive Christ. We think not, and for evidence we would like to quote an excerpt from a devotional message Roy Campbell gave before a prayer group. He said: "When my little grandson Larry was slightly over four years of age, he took the Lord Jesus as his personal Saviour. For about a year or so before that, he had shown a terrible dislike for radio broadcasts of a religious nature. When he heard a hymn over the radio he would shout 'Shut that thing off!' One day when he was convalescing from an illness, he reluctantly agreed to his grandfather's reading a gospel story to him. The story told of a little girl, about Larry's age who had accepted Christ as her personal Saviour. The grandfather realizing the appropriateness of the occasion stopped reading and said with bated breath, 'Larry.' Larry looked up. 'When I reach out my hand to you, will you take it, showing that you here and now receive the Lord Jesus

Christ as your personal Saviour?' Larry hesitated only a split second and then reached out his hand to his grandfather and said, 'Yes, I do.' Four years have passed and Larry has never once shown any dislike of hymns or religious programs to this day. He prays his own prayers, remembering always his little brother and the others in the family. Althought he still is young, it is noticeable how he leans toward God and his Saviour."

Four years have passed, and just recently Larry did something that attests to the reality of his salvation. Mr. Campbell goes on to say, "Larry and his little brother Hal, who is two and a half, were out playing in the yard. Their mother, noting the unusual silence, went out to investigate and found them both on their knees on the floor of the garden swing, heads bowed and eyes closed. As the mother approached Larry looked up and said, 'Mother, Hal's a Christian. He just gave his heart to Christ. I asked him if he would and he said, "Um-hm." ' "

Mr. Brehm says, "However great may be his joy and peace through having received the Lord Jesus Christ into his life, all too soon he is likely to be in distress as he finds thoughts, desires, and feelings within him that are anything but Christian. He is not likely to speak of them."

He may fear that his experience was but a passing emotion; or if he really was saved, that he has already lost his salvation. It is exceedingly important that he be shown from the Word that when he received Christ's life, the divine nature, he still retained the old nature, the sinful self-life with which he was born and which came to him through Adam. Also, that it is along this line in his inner life that the allurements of the world and the temptations of Satan seek to lead him astray. As he realizes the power of Satan, the world, and his own self-life, he may be tempted to give up the battle, submit to living a defeated Christian life, or even go back to the world. With nothing but failure in the face of the presence and power of sin, the only way to victory is surrender to the wonderful indwelling Saviour who alone is able to counteract the self-life. Yet what a terrific struggle so often precedes that surrender! It is surrender not only for victory over the power of sin, but surrender of the life, all that one is and has, all that he hopes to be and do, for God's use and glory.

How your child needs your prayers and counsel and encouragement at this critical time! He needs to see that his defeat makes blessed victory possible, in that he now sees how hopeless it is for him to try to keep himself in his own strength. Also, that just as fully as he rested upon Christ for his salvation, so he must trust Christ to keep him in victory over sin. This should be a very definite transaction of surrendering himself, spirit, soul, and body to Christ, that He may truly be the Lord of his life.

At the very moment of complete surrender to Christ, he should be led to take a step of faith to believe that the blessed Holy Spirit, the Spirit of Christ who came into his life when he was saved, now fills every part of his life which he has surrendered to Christ. With wise, spiritually minded parents to guide him through this exceedingly important spiritual crisis, and standing upon such Scriptures as John 7:37 and Ephesians 5:18, he is now in a position to make tremendous strides in growth in grace.

Little ten-year-old Carol Bird had great longings to be holy. Her father says: "We often spent long evenings over the Word, speaking together of the one way of deliverance from sin and self, therein so clearly revealed: a present salvation, here and now, through the death of Jesus for us and through our union with Him in that death."

The sixth chapter of Romans, and similar Scriptures,

were read and prayed over until the truth of the experience in Galatians 2:20 was realized: "I have been crucified with Christ." Of the very real and blessed experience of which her father thus speaks, we have a sweet record in the flyleaf of her Bible: "I truly *died* with Jesus, and I put away my old Carol on the cross with Him on the fourth day of October, 1903, and I mean to live by His help, for Him all my life, not I, but Christ. This was not when I was converted."

Hudson Taylor went through this terrific conflict of which Mr. Brehm speaks. Almost all Christians go through this struggle, and many never go on to real victory but "backslide" into a life of defeat, discouragement, and indifference to the things of God. But Hudson Taylor went on to realize that fullness of the Christ-Life within, and it was this realization that brought the struggle to an end.

Mr. Taylor wrote of the letter that proved to be the light-bearer he needed to resolve the deep conflict and unrest of soul: "The part specially helpful to me is: 'How then to have our faith increased? Only by thinking of all that Jesus is and all He is for us: His life, His death, His works, He Himself as revealed to us in the Word, to be the subject of our constant thoughts. Not by a striving to have faith, or to increase our faith, but a looking off to the Faithful One seems all we need.' Here, I feel, is the secret: not asking how I am to get sap out of the vine into myself, but remembering that Jesus is the vine, the root, stem, branches, twigs, leaves, flowers, fruit, all indeed. Aye, and far more too! He is the soil and sunshine, air and rain—more than we can ask, think or desire. Let us not then want to get anything out of Him, but rejoice in being ourselves in Him, one with Him, and consequently with all His fullness. Not seeking for faith to bring holiness, but rejoicing in the fact of perfect holiness in Christ let us realize that inseparably one with Him this holiness is ours, and accepting the fact, find it so indeed."

Later he said, "I have not to make myself a branch—the Lord Jesus tells me I am a branch: I am part of Him and have just to believe it and act upon it.

"If I go to the bank in Shanghai, having an account, and ask for fifty dollars, the clerk cannot refuse it to my outstretched hand and say that it belongs to Mr. Taylor. What belongs to Mr. Taylor my hand may take. It is a member of my body and I am a member of Christ and may take all I need of His fullness. I have seen it long enough in the Bible, but I believe it now as a living reality."

Hudson Taylor was anxious for his children to know early the liberating power of this great truth. Writing to Miss Blatchely, who was caring for his children he said, "I do long for them to learn early, and, once for all, the precious truths which have come so late to me concerning oneness with and the indwelling of Chirst. These do not seem to me more difficult of apprehension than the truths about redemption. Doth need the teaching of the Spirit, nothing more . . . Try to explain these most sweet and practical yet simple truths to the children, and do draw out their desire for these things. . . . 'Out of the mouths of babes and sucklings thou hast perfected praise.'

"Faithful co-operation with the Spirit in life and the daily walk will make it possible for Him to probe down into the inner recesses of the child's nature and bring to light the evil characteristics of the self-life. And with his consent, the Spirit will put them to death through the experience of his daily life (Gal. 5:24). If ever he needs the sympathetic and prayerful guidance of godly parents around the family altar, it is at this period of his experience.

"The great objective of all that has preceded this point is that the very life of Christ might be formed in him (Gal.

4:19). As he makes room in his life for the Holy Spirit, the Spirit makes room for Christ. As he permits the Spirit to crucify his self-life, the Spirit will form within him the Christ-life (Gal. 2:20). Christ will be formed in his inner life on a spiritual basis just as truly as the Lord Jesus was formed in the Virgin Mary on a physical basis."

Then as the blessed Holy Spirit makes Christ real to the heart and life we pray with unceasing desire the prayer of Mrs. C. H. Morris:

> Nearer, still nearer, close to Thy heart,
> Draw me, my Saviour, so precious Thou art;
> Fold me, oh, fold me close to Thy breast,
> Shelter me safe in that "Haven of Rest,"
> Shelter me safe in that "Haven of Rest."
>
> Nearer, still nearer, while life shall last,
> Till safe in glory my anchor is cast;
> Through endless ages, ever to be,
> Nearer, my Saviour, still nearer to Thee,
> Nearer, my Saviour, still nearer to Thee!

The whole work and objective of the Holy Spirit in His ministry to the believer is to make Christ all and in all. It is this that explains many of the otherwise strange and severe experiences God's children pass through. To show the child this "bright" side of "dark" experiences before they come to pass is the blessed privilege of parents. Abbot Kittredge in explaining this experience says: "It is a truth, which we generally learn only with added years, and as the fruit of divine chastenings, that our wealth and our happiness come not from the outside, but are a heart possession, received only from the liberal hand of a spiritual experience, and that in proportion as we are stripped of visible comforts and joys, we grow rich in inward sources of joy, which more than compensate for these light and momentary afflictions. This statement may be ridiculed by the man of the world, and may excite surprise in the mind of childhood and youth, to whose joyous vision life is one long, cloudless summer's day; but there is a large family of tried and suffering children of the Father, who know the sweet value of sorrow by the richness of the fruitage which has followed the pruning, and who can whisper through the tears, 'It was good for me that I was afflicted.' "

What are these "guests of the heart," whose voices sound clearest when the voices of earth are hushed, and in whose companionship we find a solace and balm for disappointment and trial? Memory is one of them, and with this guest we wander through all the paths of former years and hold communion with the friends of "auld lang syne," until at times we almost forget the present with its shadows, as we live in the sunshine of the past.

Hope is another guest, ever pointing to the brightness which comes after the storm, to the rest which will be sweeter after the weariness, to the reunion of loving hearts in the home where links are never broken since "no one ever goes out." And with memory and hope as guests within, the face of the one turned backward to the joys that once were ours, the face of the other illumined with the glory of the joys of the near future, the paths we are treading grow less rough and dreary, and we begin to sing even "in the night."

Peace is another guest, and the deeper the waves of sorrow, the more precious does this guest become. The ocean has its tempest-tossed billows, which seem mad in their fury, but only the ocean has its quiet depths far below the billows, unruffled by the storm. The Christian's peace is not in the absence of waves of sorrow, but it is a profound calm which is experienced only under the waves.

Aspiration is another guest. When we walk in the sunshine of worldly prosperity, self-love too often absorbs our thoughts, and we are content with our earthly possessions, thinking little of spiritual beauty and power. But sorrow turns the eyes away from self, by robbing us of these possessions, and then out of the desolateness of our souls arise longings for a higher, grander soul-life, and we learn the rich meaning of the prayer, "Nearer, my God, to Thee! Nearer to Thee!" and thus, upon the rounds of our grief, we climb up toward the perfect stature of a complete sanctification.

But of all the "guests of the heart," the chief, the most beautiful, is Jesus, the heart's King, the Elder Brother. And sorrow reveals His preciousness, perfects His fellowship, makes His love a soft pillow and a rapturous joy. Surrounded by human friendship, satisfied with earthly riches, Jesus is only valued prospectively, for what He will be in death and in the judgment. But when earthly supports are taken away and we lean hard upon Him, then we know His sustaining strength. When in the silence of bereavement we cry, "Speak, Lord, for thy servant heareth," then we know the richness of His comfort and the fullness of His grace. It was through the experience of the "loss of all things" that Paul grew up into the mighty passion of that cry of love, "That I may know him." And so God in every age has stripped His children of one earthly treasure after another until the burdened heart has had "Jesus only" to rest upon, and then "Jesus only" has become the heart's passionate longing; to know Him, the loss of all things has seemed a joyous privilege. In the fellowship of this divine Guest of the heart, we shall find our heaven begun below, a heaven whose perfect bliss will be ours when awaking in His likeness we behold Him "face to face." Till then, we will covet the sorrows which bring

Him closer to our hearts and through whose chastening we grow up into His likeness.

Let the young seek the fellowship of the godly. How fortunate are those youth who have the inestimable blessing of living in a godly family, hearing and hearkening daily (in the family altar) to a wise man's learning (Prov. 16:23; I Kings 10:8); or who are in fellowship with a true, Bible-believing church where each imparts from his store of divine wisdom for the increase and edifying of the members of Christ's Body (Eph. 4:15, 16; Acts 2:42; Heb. 10:24). How vitally important that our young people be taught from the tenderest years around the family altar and on all possible opportune occasions to be in fellowship with those who fear God and keep His commandments (Ps. 119:63; cf Prov. 19:16; 2:20)!

Service

The child should be trained for service. The precious values of salvation are not to be selfishly enjoyed, but are to be passed on to others by faithful witnessing, deeds of kindness, and words of encouragement. The Christian is to be first a possessor, then a bearer, and lastly a sharer. No blessing reaches its fulfillment in a life until it is shared with another needy life. The apostle Paul, writing to the Corinthians, said, "O ye Corinthians, our mouth is open unto you, our heart is enlarged" (II Cor. 6:11). The apostle's heart and life was opened to share his blessings with the needs of others; he was not closed up to a selfish enjoyment of God's blessing, thus to become a dead sea with every blessing turned to bitterness and corruption.

TRUST

A picture memory brings to me;
I look across the years and see
Myself beside my mother's knee.

I feel her gentle hand restrain
My selfish moods, and know again
A child's blind sense of wrong and pain.

But wiser now, a man gray grown,
My childhood's needs are better known;
My mother's chastening love I own.

Gray grown, but in our Father's sight
A child still groping for the light
To read His works and ways aright.

I bow myself beneath His hand:
That pain itself for good was planned,
I trust, but cannot understand.

I fondly dream it needs must be
That as my mother dealt with me,
So with His children dealeth He.

I wait and trust the end will prove
That here and there, below, above,
The chastening heals, the pain is love!

—John G. Whittier.

8

FUNDAMENTAL PRINCIPLES OF
CHILD TRAINING

BEGIN EARLY. 1. The earlier the training the more effective it will be. Bridges says: "It is a matter of experience that what is early learnt is most firmly retained. It stands the friction of time with the least injury. Far better, instead of waiting for the maturity of reason, to work upon the pliability of childhood. The gardener begins to graft in the first rising of the sap. If the crooked shoots of self will and disobedience are not cut off, their rapid growth and rapidly growing strength will greatly increase the future difficulty of bending them. Present neglect occasions after [later] risk and great future perplexity. We may begin our work too late, but we can scarcely begin it too soon (see Eccles. 11:6; Isa. 28:9, 10; Lam. 3:27). If the child be too young to teach to read, he cannot be too young to teach to obey. Never let the watchfulness to check the buddings of evil and to cherish the first tenderness of right feeling be relaxed. The ceaseless activity of the great enemy teaches the value of early training. Be beforehand with him. Preoccupy the ground with good seed, as the most effectual exclusion of his evil tares. Be at the very beginning of the way with wholesome food, ere Satan has the opportunity of pouring in his 'bread of deceit' ere nature is hardened by the habits of sin—brutalized by familiarity with vice."

2. The training must be practical. Mere talk about Christ that is sandwiched in at irregular intervals is neither prac-

tical nor effective. Mere talk to a child about the Word of God without bringing it to bear upon his loose habits and self-willed tempers is utterly ineffective. Hannah began her training of Samuel with his dedication to God, and then prayed the prayer that every mother and father should daily pray: "How shall we order the child, and how shall we do unto him?" (Judg. 13:12). Hannah wanted to train her child in a practical way and with effective results.

If the child's training in the Word of God (II Tim. 3:15-17) is to be effective, the child must observe consistency in his parents. They must be what they say. Their words must be answered to by their lives.

3. Be patient. Sometimes the fruit of a child's training is immediate, rich, and permanent to the end (see I Sam. 1:28; 2:26; 12:2, 3; cf. Ps. 92:13-15). But often the bread cast upon the waters is found not till "after many days" (Eccles. 11:1)—perhaps not till after the godly parent has gone to heaven. Yet the fruit, thought late, will not be less sure (Hab. 2:3). Pastor John Flavel has said, "It is no small mercy [alluding to his own case] to have thousands of fervent prayers lying before the Lord, filled up in heaven for us."

The child may in some cases (we believe these cases will be few indeed) depart when he is young; but when he is old, smothered convictions will bring back the power of early impressions. The seeds of instruction sown in the early and tender years will without any doubt burst forth into life. The Scriptures early bound on his memory will force themselves upon him many a time and with many a sharp and painful thrust. Conscience so trained will disturb his sinful pleasures and embitter all the sweetness which he had found or hoped to find in his sins. The remembrance of his parents' godly house will one day bring the prodigal "to himself," and he will come home with shame, tears, and godly sorrow (Luke 15:17-20).

4. Be in faith—nothing doubting. Let parents cultivate daily the sweet exercise of faith, trusting not to what is seen but to what God has promised; in some cases even like our father Abraham, "against hope, believing in hope" (Rom. 4:18-20). Expect the fulfillment of Proverbs 22:6 as much as any other promise of the gospel. If your children observe you moving about them with a bright, immovable faith for their souls' obedience to the Lord, they will be deeply affected for good by such faith and expectancy. If they see gloom, doubt, and fear they will be adversely affected, and the powers of Satan will have a grip more firmly fixed upon their souls. Let us remember that the children tend to become just what we expect of them.

With such rich promises in God's Word, every faithful parent has an abundant basis for a bright faith and a fervent expectancy for the very best for his children spiritually. God has promised, "I will be a God to thee, and to thy seed after thee. I will pour out my Spirit upon thy seed, and my blessing upon thy offspring" (see II Cor. 1:20; Gen. 17:7; Isa. 44:3-5). Bridges has a most beautiful passage concerning the promise in Proverbs 22:6. He tells us we can expect the fulfillment of Proverbs 22:6 as well as the fulfillment of John 6:37. Observe his beautiful analysis: "John 6:37 is couched in the same grammatical terms—a promise connected with a duty, as the encouragement to the duty: 'Him that cometh—he that traineth; in no wise cast out—will not depart,' yet the latter (Prov. 22:6) is often considered a general promise, admitting of various and indefinite exceptions. The other (John 6:37) is 'Yea and Amen.' But we might ask, How can we loosen the ground of one promise without shaking the foundation of all? And do not admitted exceptions to the educational promise give occasion to many an exercised Christian to find his own exception in the gospel promise? We fully concede that the ground here is more clear to the exercise of faith. We have the demonstrable certainty of the work of the Son, the faithfulness of the Father and the agency of the Spirit, drawing the 'given to come' (vv. 37, 44, 65) the compact of the Eternal Three unchangeably fulfilled. *In this parental promise the manifestly imperfect training of the parent, and the wanton rebellion of the child, obscures the ground of faith to our vision.*

"But this touches only the apprehension of the ground, not the ground itself. If the performance of the parent's duty in the one promise were as certain as the work of God in the other, would not the assurance of the promise in both cases be equally firm? Is it not far safer and more satisfactory to take all the promises of the Bible upon the *same* ground? The cases that appear to contradict the educational promise (Prov. 22:6) seem to be fairly explained. Not that the promise is falsified, but that the Lord's time of fulfillment is not yet come. Or has not some important element of education been omitted? Has not some disproportion of one or other part of the system hindered the efficiency of the whole? Has instruction and discipline been always accompanied with prayer and faith? Or has prayer been always confirmed by consistent practice? Does not man's indolence, self-indulgence, unbelief, unfaithfulness to the conditions implied, wither the blessing? While Abraham— training up his family for God—shall find Him 'faithful that hath promised' (cf. Gen. 18:19 with Heb. 10:23), the Elis and the Davids—*good men* but *bad parents* (I Sam. 3:13; I Kings 1:16)—shall know 'God's breach of promise' (Num. 14:23). It is too deep for man to reconcile the absolute election of God with weak, imperfect, unfaithful fulfillment of duty. Nevertheless in all cases—'Let God be true, and every man a liar' (Rom. 3:4)."

FOR A DISOBEDIENT CHILD

Look down, O mighty Searcher of the soul,
   Upon my wayward, disobedient child
And drive away perverse and sinful tempers,
   From this young heart; without Thy Holy Spirit,
Strengthening our better wishes and instilling
   Heaven-seeking thoughts, all hopeless were the struggle
Between our passions and our good resolves;
   Be near with thy assisting grace, I pray Thee,
To this poor wanderer from the path of peace;
   And pour upon the sin-tormented breast
The soothing medicine of contrite love;
   And this be mine, blest happy talk indeed!
With kind and gentle words to tell how pardon
   Is offered here on earth, how help is given
To the sincerely penitent to curb
   Each evil tendency with hope of heaven,
For His dear sake whose death our ransom paid,
   And in whose name my every prayer is made.

9

DISCIPLINE

SOMEONE HAS SAID that discipline is a lost word in the vocabulary of our generation. Yet discipline is required in the life of a child if he is to be well established spiritually, moderate emotionally, socially adjusted and happy personally. The Word of God has guidance for us at this point, and as we study His Book we shall be thankful for the wise guidance He has afforded us on this important question.

Spanking is one form of discipline, and a very necessary form. In Proverbs 13:24 God says, "He that spareth his rod hateth his son; but he that loveth him chasteneth him betimes."

Faithful discipline in the way of the rod will spare the child heart-breaking experiences later in life. Later God is constrained by His love to do this job that in many cases should have been cared for by the parents (Ps. 39:10; I Peter 5:6).

"God will," as one old writer says, "wither their brightest comforts—children, property, talents, friendships—if they turn them to idols; and this not for His pleasure but for their profit (Heb. 12:10; cf. Lam. 3:33); and how many have not blessed Him that He did not refrain His discipline until it had done its perfect work?"

God says foolishness is bound up in the heart of a child (Prov. 22:15; Gen. 8:21). All choose from the very beginning of life the broad road that leads to destruction (Isa.

53:6). We should note God says *foolishness*, not *childishness*. Childishness is no sin, but foolishness is. Foolishness manifests itself in different ways: now as the passion of anger; now a willfulness that would despise all that crosses the personal will; now as selfishness, grasping greedily to satisfy self and ignoring the claims and needs of others. We might say that foolishness means selfishness that issues forth as a determination to have our own way irrespective of the will of God and of others; and when willfullness is frustrated it quickly becomes anger and hatred. Augustine mentions his being struck with the sight of an infant before it could speak, showing an evident look of envy and passion toward another infant about to share its nourishment. He adds, in reference to himself, "When, I beseech Thee, O my God, in what places—when or where—was I innocent?" (Confessions 1.c.7).

Satan begins with the infant in arms (Ps. 58:3; Isa. 48:8). The violent cry of passion is the first evident sin of Adam's corruption. Vigilant spiritual training must begin as early. Every vice begins in seed form in the nursery. The secret is to establish authority in the dawn of life; to bend the tender twig before it is a mighty oak and beyond our power (Eccles. 12:1, 2). Self-will must be broken in the very beginning. (See chapter, "The Christian Mother.") The child must be made to obey. The child's self-will must not be yielded to either to appease his anger or his crying. In either case the child gets the idea that he can "get his way" by being disagreeable, and it then becomes practically impossible to break self-will. Willfulness, when denied, seeks to force and coerce satisfaction of its desire by the violence of hatred and anger or by crying. If willfulness is yielded to under either of these forms, the personality of the child will ever after seek to satisfy its willfulness by being as disagreeable as possible. This behavior pattern can frequently be noted in adults who confess, as life refuses to yield to them, that they are most miserable and unhappy people.

The rod is to be used for the purpose of inflicting pain on the willful child. The pain is inflicted that the child might early learn that pain is the price life exacts of the selfish and willful.

The child is thus saved from the false notion that life will sanction or reward willfulness and disobedience. The pain he suffers will cause him to give up the way of life which draws the pain and suffering upon him. Being faithfully taught early in life the child will be spared the tragedy of hardening into selfishness and willfulness which in later life would be well-nigh impossible to break. An old divine has written:

"Insurmountable indeed is the difficulty when the child has been allowed to become the early master. When the habit of disobedience has been formed and hardened it is almost impossible to then break the spirit of disobedience. God's word says, 'It is good for a man if he bear the yoke in his youth' (Lam. 3:27)."

Sentimental kindness to the children in their disobedience is a great sin that will plague and curse their lives. "Eli could not have devised which way to have plagued himself and his house so much, as by his kindness to his children's sin. Parents need no other means of making themselves miserable than by sparing the rod." So wrote the great Bishop Hall in his *Contemplations* (Book 11.vii). Scripture reveals plainly the bitter sorrow that comes from winking and passing over the child's disobedience. Read and ponder Proverbs 29:15; I Samuel 3:13; I Kings 1:6; 2:25 and compare with II Samuel 13:39.

Bridges says on Proverbs 22:15: "Observe the rooted character of this evil. *It is bound in his heart*—held firmly there by chains invincible to human power (cf. Gen. 44:30, 31; I Sam. 18:1). It is woven and incorporated into his very nature, and so various are its forms, so subtle its workings, that the wisest parent is often at a loss how to detect and treat the evil. The general rule however—the prescribed remedy—is clear. It is vain to bid the foolishness depart. It is no less vain to persuade the child himself to drive it far away. The rod of correction is distinctly named, and repeatedly inculcated, as God's own means for this important end (Prov. 19:18; 23:13, 14; 29:17). Only let the child see that, as with our heavenly Father, love is the ruling principle (Prov. 13:24, with 3:11, 12); that we follow the example of the wisest and best of parents; that we use His rod for driving foolishness away (see II Chron. 33:12, 13)."

Prayer, the family altar, counsel, pleading, moral axioms, all of it and none of it will *substitute* for this God-appointed means! We may not claim we are fulfilling Proverbs 22:6, if we are ignoring Proverbs 22:15. There is more than chastening in Proverbs 22:6, but there is not less.

"Let it [the rod] not be used at all times. Let remonstrance be first tried; like our heavenly Father, who will never stir the rod with His children if His still small voice of instruction prevails. Magnifying trifles into grave offenses, chiding every slip of childishness or troublesome forgetfulness, casts a baneful gloom upon the home. It is 'a continual dropping in a very rainy day' (Prov. 27:15). This *indiscriminate* correction soon brings a callous deadness to all sense of shame. Let it be reserved, at least in its more serious forms, for *willfulness*. It is *medicine,* not food. It is the remedy for *constitutional* diseases, not the daily diet for life and nourishment. And to convert medicine into food gradually destroys its remedial qualities.

"Some parents use nothing but correction. They indulge

their own passions at the expense of their less guilty children. Unlike our heavenly Father, they afflict and grieve their children willingly (contrast Lam. 3:33; Heb. 12:10) to vent their own anger not to subdue their children's sins. This intemperate use of a scriptural ordinance brings discredit upon its efficacy, sows the seed of much bitter fruit; engendering in their children a spirit of bondage and concealment, sometimes of disgust and even of hatred toward their unreasonable parents. 'If parents,' said a wise and godly father (Matthew Henry) 'would not correct their children except in a praying frame when they can "lift up their heads without wrath," it would neither provoke God nor them.' Other parents freely threaten the rod, yet without using it. It was only meant to frighten. Many parents scare, but they touch not and in reality leave the child to go his own way of ruin (cf. I Kings 1:6-9; 2:23-25). It soon becomes an empty sound, powerless and hardening. God's threatenings are not vain words. If His children will not turn, they will find His warnings faithful and true. This threatening play is solemn trifling with truth; teaching children by example what they had learned from the womb (Ps. 58:3)—to speak lies. Let our words be considerate but certain" (Bridges).

No chastening is for the present joyous but grievous (Heb. 12:11); yet when given in prayer, wisdom, and faith it is ordained for the pain of the flesh that the soul may be delivered from hell and ungodliness (cf. I Cor. 5:5; 11:32).

Indeed, the purpose and plan of chastening is threefold: For their profit (Heb. 12:10); for their *promotion* in holiness (Heb. 12:10); and for the production of godly traits (Heb. 12:11). When chastening is faithfully administered by the parents, together with daily instruction of the child that he may daily be occupied with *looking unto Jesus* (Heb. 12:2), the three-fold result is certain. Swincock in

Christian Man's Calling said, "Lord, do Thou be pleased to strike in with every stroke, that the rod of correction may be a rod of instruction." Bishop Hall said, "It is a rare soul that can be kept in constant order without smarting remedies. I confess mine cannot. How wild had I run, if the rod had not been over me? Every man can say he thanks God for his ease. For me, I bless God for my trouble" *(Silent Thoughts)*.

Popular psychology has frequently been at a loss to find a place for "the rod" in the discipline of the child. The reason for this is because of a weakness in popular psychology itself. Popular psychology looks everywhere for the causes of human misbehavior except to the perverted will of the violator himself. They seek to find all causes in the emotions or the intellect, but they have missed the will and so have ignored that faculty of man which would yield the key to the problem of maladjustment and misbehavior in personalities. Thus the psychologist speaks of "missing the mark" as a disease, whereas the Christian speaks of it as sin. The Christian recognizes the part the emotions and intellect play in maladjustment and misbehavior, yet he goes deeper and recognizes the key to the problem is in a perverse will, issuing forth in a willing and willfulness that is concerned chiefly with self-satisfaction and is in utter rebellion against those demands, duties, and responsibilities, those situations and events of life that deny selfish desires and satisfactions.

After one theologian had read a popular treatise by a well-known psychologist, he was asked his view of the treatise. He replied, "Much that the psychologist says is true, but he does not go deep enough. His views of man are too shallow and surfaced. He has not gone deep enough to recognize the perverse willfulness and antisocial, anti-God selfishness that is at the heart of man and his problem of maladjustment and misbehavior, or just plain sin, as we theologians say."

It is because man is born with a perverse selfishness and thus a perverse willfulness that the severe form of discipline, such as the rod, is necessary.

Yet, while we recognize the perverse factor in the child, we must recognize as he grows older that all disobedience will not be due to a perverse willfulness but may also be due to emotional frustrations, lack of understanding, and ignorance. Discipline in these cases will take the form of counseling, kindness, and love. The attempt will be made by the parents to understand the child and to remove the cause of his difficulties. As a case in point we would quote from a recent article in the *Evangelical Beacon* by Professor Milford Sholund.

"One day I was asked to teach a group of boys less than ten years of age. There were about seven active lads in the class. Each of them seemed normal and happy in his relationship to the children in the department. But my delight soon became a disappointment. One of the younger boys who was unusually large gave a small girl a sharp push in the small of her back. She went sprawling and crying across the floor. I immediately laid hands on the boy and tried to shake some sense into him. He only looked at me and grinned wryly. He sat down quietly at my side as the worship service continued. In a moment I noticed that my husky blonde challenger had scooted from one chair to the next and suddenly boosted one of the chairs in front of him. An innocent girl fell from her chair. My 'problem' pupil only grinned. When the worship service was concluded with prayer, the boys dashed hither and thither grabbing chairs to carry into their class session. Finally teacher and pupil were somewhat in order in the room set apart for them. But peace was to be ours only a minute.

"The little 'strong man' twisted the arm of a 'good little' boy. The victim seemed bewildered and beaten. His big-muscle conqueror gloated in his strength. Needless to say, the class session was thoroughly disturbed with earnest exhortations and vain efforts by the teacher. The Sunday morning of Christian education left me wondering what could be done for this Scandinavian lad who had misdirected his energies in Sunday school.

"My good wife suggested that one way of learning more about this troublesome pupil would be to invite him for dinner the next Sunday. We called his parents. They seemed to appreciate the Sunday school, especially its interest in their boy.

"The following Sunday the young challenger appeared in Sunday school with abounding energy and a responsive smile. He behaved well in the Sunday school worship service and class period. He spoke freely of his anticipation of a good time at our home. His social adjustment in our house was good. He ate well and played happily with the children. His outdoor activity was somewhat daring and rough, but he was attentive to a word of caution. When we told him that it was time to go home, he seemed anxious to stay longer. The investment of time, dinner, and effort had already won a friend. The problem of discipline was beginning to be resolved through kindness. Our young friend insisted that we meet his parents as we drove nearer to his home.

"We found his home to be well-furnished. His parents were cordial, but evidently not interested in attending church. We learned later that the husband had made an idol of his work. He was too busy to either play or pray with his boy. Now he was paying heavily in the heartaches of a son who confronted his parents with disobedience. We also learned through the visit that the boy's mother was rather cool in her affection for him. She often threatened the boy with corporal punishment by the father. The final admission of poor relationships in the home came when the mother indicated that the only time the father paid attention to the boy was when he was scolding or punishing him.

"This energetic, healthy boy continues to come to Sunday school. He has outbursts of temper. But the secret of his life is not opened through discipline that sternly rebukes and attempts of coerce him. What he wants and needs is love that warms his heart.

"My wife taught the class one day in my absence. Our 'problem pupil'—more correctly, 'our pupil with problems'—again had his fit of trouble. She took him into a separate room and spoke to him of his trouble-making. Then she said, 'My, but you are a good-looking boy!' At once he relaxed and smiled affectionately. His Sunday school teacher had praised him and won him. Someone really cared enough to notice him. He showed the same response as the poor little boy who sat in the rain on the steps of the Sunday school in the Free Church in Portland and confessed to his pals, 'The reason I like this Sunday school so much is because they love you so much.'

"Paul said the goodness of God leads us to repentance. Jesus disciplined His own through love. When every other technique of discipline fails, remember love never fails (I Cor. 13)."

With rare poetic skill, Robert Burns paints a picture of a family group at worship in *The Cotter's Saturday Night:*

The priest-like father reads the sacred page,
How Abraham was the friend of God on high;

Or, Moses bade eternal warfare wage
With Amalek's ungracious progeny;
Or how the royal bard did groaning lie
Beneath the stroke of Heaven's avenging ire;
Or Job's pathetic plaint, and wailing cry;
Or rapt Isaiah's wild, seraphic fire;
  Or other holy seers that tune the sacred lyre.

Perhaps the Christian volume is the theme,
How guiltless blood for guilty man was shed;
How He, who bore in heaven the second name,
Had not on earth whereon to lay His head;
How His first followers and servants sped,
The precepts sage they wrote to many a land;
How he who lone in Patmos banished,
Saw in the sun a mighty Angel stand;

  And heard great Bab'lon's doom pronounc'd by Heaven's
    command.

Then kneeling down, to heaven's Eternal King,
The saint, the father, and the husband prays:
Hope "springs exulting on triumphant wing,"
That thus they all shall meet in future days:
There ever bask in uncreated rays,
No more to sigh, or shed the bitter tear,
Together hymning their Creator's praise,
In such society, yet still more dear:
  While circling Time moves round in an eternal sphere.

Compar'd with this, how poor Religion's pride,
In all the pomp of method and of art,
When men display to congregations wide
Devotion's ev'ry grace, except the heart!
The Pow'r, incens'd, the pageant will desert,
The pompous strain, the sacerdotal stole;

But haply, in some cottage far apart,
May hear, well pleased, the language of the soul;
  And in His Book of Life the inmates poor enroll.

Then homeward all take off their sev'ral way;
The youngling cottagers retire to rest:
The parent-pair their secret homage pay,
And proffer up to Heaven the warm request,
That He, who stills the raven's clam'rous nest,
And decks the lily fair in flow'ry pride,
Would, in the way his wisdom sees the best,
For them and for their little ones provide;
  But, chiefly, in their hearts with grace divine preside.

From scenes like these old Scotia's grandeur springs,
That makes her lov'd at home, revered abroad:
Princes and lords are but the breath of kings,
"An honest man's the noblest work of God."

. . . .

10

THE FAMILY ALTAR—THE
CHIEF MEANS OF INSTRUCTION

Matthew 18:20

M ALTBIE BABCOCK has challenged: "Dare we let children
grow up with no vital contact with the Saviour, never
intentionally and consciously put into His arms? Not to
bring them to Him, not to teach them to walk toward Him,
as soon as they can walk toward anyone, is wronging a
child beyond words. The terrible indictment uttered by
the Lord—'Them that were entering in ye hindered,' and
the millstone warning for offending little ones, are close
akin to the deserts of them who ruin a man's whole day
of life by wronging his morning hours. Not to help a
child to know the saving power of Christ is to hold back
a man from salvation."

Read and ponder Mark 9:36, 37.

Children must be taught. Start early. Let God's Word
fall upon their minds and hearts from the earliest day. Trust
the Holy Spirit to root it there by His wisdom, even though
the child himself has as yet no thinking powers to hold it.
The rod will not be needed so much as some might fear if
faithful, daily instruction of the young from the earliest
days is attended to! Only divine wisdom can give the
fear and knowledge of God (Prov. 2:5), a principle of
practical godliness (Prov. 2:7-9), a preservation from be-
setting temptations (Prov. 2:10-19), and guidance into the
right and safe path (Prov. 2:20).

It is first of all *the word in the heart* (not head) that is effective. Babies may have the Word dropped into their hearts long before they can secure it in their heads. God instructs us that His Word sown in the heart does work to mold the whole life (Prov. 24:13, 14; Job 23:12; Ps. 119:103; Jer. 15:16).

Rather than the head then passing the Word on to the heart (as we are so prone to believe in this shallow age), may not the true direction be the other way—the heart passing the Word on up to the head with such living power through the Holy Spirit as to strike all the faculties of the mind with burning conviction? We definitely think so! Long before a child begins to think, he has been in daily association with sights and sounds. These daily associations form the background against which he later begins to form thoughts. Let us be wise and take a cue here. Let the child's heart, ears, and eyes be filled with the Word of God before he is able to think. Then as the process of thinking begins to function, his thoughts will have these impressions, hearings, sights, heart-movings there to guide his thinking and to mark its tone and direction! A mother heard her little baby say a curse word before he ever had much of an idea if any what it meant! The thinking was not there, but the sense impression was! Naturally, as he begins to think, his thoughts will follow these words, the sound- and sense-impressions he has heard. In other words he will draw the meaning out of what he already has by way of sense and emotional impression. Most babies are full of the world from the beginning; no wonder they start thinking that way, so far away from God!

We feed baby before he has the least idea what food is for. But his body is so made that it takes the food and turns it into energy which can be later turned into brain power. Why not feed him God's Word before he has any idea what it's all about? His *impressionable* little soul will take it, and that little heart somehow by God's power holds the sights, sounds, and impressions of His Word and turns it into divine energizings that can later be turned into thoughts and ideas.

The truth of the matter is this: a child may be impressed long before he has the power to express. He has the power to receive impressions long before he has the power of thinking and understanding. From the moment of birth he is a little bundle of life that is receiving impressions, through the eye-gate, ear-gate, and heart-gate; what he hears, sees, and feels is stored up in his heart; and as he begins to think his expressions will draw up and out of his impressions. His impressions provide the mold into which his thoughts and interests will be cast.

The whole point of the early training (in the pre-thinking state) is to prepare the mold, to prepare him for thinking and understanding so that when this stage comes he will from the beginning think the thoughts of God after Him. Remember Jesus said, "Out of the heart are the issues of life."

We pour God's Word into our babies for the same reason the builder brings his tools and materials to the site of a building project: so that they will be there when he is ready to begin work.

Talk about impressions! Doctors tell us that a baby for nine months before he is born is being impressed and influenced for good or ill by the actions, moods, thoughts, and feelings of the mother. The life is being influenced and the mold for later thoughts, actions, and decisions is being laid by the mother even before birth! In the Word of God this is confirmed: "And it came to pass, that, when Elisabeth heard the salutation of Mary, the babe leaped in her womb; and Elisabeth was filled with the Holy Ghost" (Luke 1:41).

Now the real question is not, Can he receive the impressions of God's word, but, Will we give it?

When the Word is poured into the baby it works on him, in him, and through him. In Hebrews 4:12, 13 we read, "For the word of God is quick, and powerful, and sharper than any twoedged sword, piercing even to the dividing asunder of soul and spirit, and of the joints and marrow, and is a discerner of the thoughts and intents of the heart. Neither is there any creature that is not manifest in his sight: but all things are naked and opened unto the eyes of him with whom we have to do."

The Word is a sword, and it can cut and pierce before the age of reason; cutting and piercing have no need to wait upon reason. How this should enlighten and encourage every parent in his faithful labor in the Word of God to his children. The greatest tragedy in Christendom and to the cause of Christ is the *utter waste of the first four golden years of opportunity*. The child in the tender, plastic, impressionable state he is in from one day to four years is the golden opportunity for every parent to lay the Word of God deep in his life as a firm foundation for all else that shall follow. Be a missionary of this wonderful truth to young married couples and those contemplating marriage. There are very few parents who realize the importance of these years.

We recall a little lad of two years in Waterloo, Iowa. He had been trained as we are advocating here, "from birth on," around the family altar. Result? One day he was asked to say grace at the table. While he was praying, verse after verse of Scripture flowed from his lips. His parents had impressed these verses at family worship during the preceding two years. They had little idea but that most of the verses had gone in one ear and out the other. But that day they found out that their little boy had heard them and retained them. Two years old and saved—full of Scripture and evidencing a real burden and desire for the salvation of his unsaved relatives. Is this a miracle? It is, but not one that cannot be repeated by every other born-again parent in the lives of his children! How? By faithful planting of the Word of God from the very beginning of the child's life. Not only believe this, reader, but practice it and see God honor you and your child beyond your greatest expectations!

The family altar is the great instrument of "instruction" in the Word of God. Philip Henry was zealous and earnest in his practice of family devotion. Besides the regular plan of reading and expounding the Scriptures morning and evening, he used strongly to recommend singing, saying that it was a way of exhibiting godliness, like Rahab's scarlet thread, to such as pass by our windows (Josh. 2:18; Ps. 118:15). His children and servants used to take notes of his family altar expositions; and the foundation of Matthew Henry's Commentary was laid from these notes. On Thursday evening, instead of reading, he used to catechize his children and servants upon the Assembly's Catechism; or else they read and he examined them in the Word of God. On Saturday evening they gave him an account of what they could remember of the chapters they had read through during the week, each a portion in order.

Philip Henry advised his children that they should take a verse of Psalm 119 every morning to meditate upon, and so go over the Psalm twice in a year. "And that" said he, "will bring you to be in love with all the rest of Scripture."

Besides this he also had days of humiliation with his family. The consequence was that, in addition to the blessings resulting to his own children, many who came to live with them dated their first impressions from these services and gave God thanks that they ever came under his roof.

No one has written with more conviction regarding the need of Christian nurture and home-training in the knowledge of God than has J. Edgar Hoover. "More and more children are being led toward crime as parents throw away responsibility. Selfishness is often the keynote of the day, and materialism the inspiration for living. God, in many instances, is not accepted in the home, and concepts of morality have been relegated to the junk heap.

"Can a nation exist void of all religious thought and action? Can we have internal peace without morality? Can we build homes without God, or have worthy parents who do not know and practice His teachings?

"The key to these problems—to life itself—is God. He is man's first need, his final goal.

"Our nation is sadly in need of a rebirth of the simple life—a return to the days when God was part of each household, when families arose in the morning with a prayer on their lips, and ended the day by gathering together to place themselves in His care.

"If there is hope for the future of America; if there is to be peace and happiness in our homes, then we as a nation must return to God and to the practice of daily family prayer.

"Our generation, it seems, has allowed old, faithful religious practices to slip into oblivion. As a result, family life has been weakened. The nation has suffered, and many of its children have become like the man whose house is built upon sand; it is an inviting ground for moral decay and crime.

"My hope for the future of this nation is predicated upon the faith in God which is nurtured in the family. No outside influence of a constructive nature can overcome the lack of a guiding light in the home, and the spark of this light must be the knowledge of God; the fuel must be the strength of prayer.

"The greatest thing we as individuals can do for ourselves and for our country will be to keep our families together in peace and happiness. There is no better way of doing our part for home-life in America than by establishing the daily practice of family prayer in our homes; because families that pray together stay together."

The power of the daily family altar to tie a family together in love and holiness is well illustrated by a testimony recently read.

"I was a guest in the house of comparative strangers, and as we came out to the dining room I noticed there was some confusion and slight embarrassment; but I was asked to return thanks and the breakfast went on.

"The next morning the father said, 'We have made you one of the family now, and before we sit down I am going to tell you just how things are. You see, we do not have much time for our family worship, but it is a rule that there must be an unbroken circle at the breakfast table. Before we sit down, each one of the family, commencing with four-year-old Jimmy, repeats a verse of Scripture, after which we join hands around the table and repeat the Lord's Prayer; then I say a few words of prayer.'

"After this explanation Jimmy started off with, 'Suffer little children to come unto me, and forbid them not, for of such is the kingdom of heaven.'

"I learned later that the four-year-old was allowed to say the same verse for a month; that the ones under eight (Oh, yes, they had them all ages, as there were ten) must have a new verse every week; over twelve there must be a new verse every morning and it must not be repeated within thirty days.

"A few months after that I was in a university town,

and there I met the oldest son of the family. I said to him, 'A fine family you have back in the old home town.'

" 'Yes, sir,' and his eyes lighted with pleasure.

"After talking with him a few minutes I said, 'Would you mind telling me what you miss most now that you are away from home?'

"The boy hesitated a moment. It is not easy for a boy of that age to unveil the deepest feelings of his heart. Then, though a deep flush showed beneath his tan and freckles, he looked straight into my eyes, and replied, 'It is the handclasp at the breakfast table. If I could feel my father's warm clasp, and repeat with them the Lord's Prayer, it would start the day off right, and nothing would matter then!'

"Again he hesitated but finished manfully, with a trace of huskiness in his voice, 'The memory of those mornings at home stand between me and many a temptation; it keeps me going straight.' "

FOR HER HUSBAND

Eternal Guardian of the good and true,
　　Before whose altar my first bridal vows
Were pledged, whose blessing sanctified the bonds
　　That joined our beating hearts; oh! God! I thank Thee
That he, the dear one that Thou gavest me then,
　　My life companion, at my side still walks;
Keep him, I pray, a thousand times I pray Thee,
　　Keep him in body and in soul, increase his faith and
Guide his footsteps in Thy way, whate'er his earthly lot,
　　　　or good, or evil;
Give him a gentle and contented heart
　　And teach him still to prize my best endeavors
To sweeten life for him and guard his love;
　　And still as time rolls onward, and life loses
The bloom and fragrance of it's earlier days,
　　O'er the brown autumn and the hoary winter
Of our declining age, pour the bright sunshine
　　Of hope and peace ineffable. Thus lead us
On to one quiet grave; then, in Thy mercy
　　Take our world-wearied souls to dwell with Thee,
Where doubt and sorrow never more can come;
　　And He, who for my sins from heaven came down
To wear the robe of scorn and thorny crown,
　　To bear His heavy cross, then hang and bleed
And die for me, 'tis in His name I plead.

　　　　　　　　　Wife's Manual, Rev. W. Calvert